Adaptations in the
Sound Era: 1927–37

Adaptations in the Sound Era: 1927–37

Deborah Cartmell

Bloomsbury Academic
An imprint of Bloomsbury Publishing Inc

BLOOMSBURY

NEW YORK · LONDON · NEW DELHI · SYDNEY

Bloomsbury Academic

An imprint of Bloomsbury Publishing Inc

1385 Broadway	50 Bedford Square
New York	London
NY 10018	WC1B 3DP
USA	UK

www.bloomsbury.com

BLOOMSBURY and the Diana logo are trademarks of Bloomsbury Publishing Plc

First published 2015

Library of Congress Cataloging-in-Publication Data
Cartmell, Deborah.
Adaptations in the sound era, 1927-37 / Deborah Cartmell.
pages cm. – (Bloomsbury adaptation histories)
Summary: "Tracks and reflects on the presence and marketing of 'words' in the early
sound era, from adaptations of Shakespeare and 19th Century novels, to biopics"–
Provided by publisher.
Includes bibliographical references and index.
ISBN 978-1-62356-042-3 (hardback) – ISBN 978-1-62356-878-8 (paperback)
1. Sound in motion pictures. 2. Sound motion pictures.
3. Literature–Adaptations–History and criticism. 4. Film adaptations–History and criticism.
5. Motion pictures–History–20th century. 6. Motion pictures–Aesthetics. I. Title.
PN1995.7.C335 2015
791.4302'4–dc23
2015000843

ISBN: HB: 978-1-6235-6042-3
PB: 978-1-6235-6878-8
ePub: 978-1-6235-6202-1
ePDF: 978-1-6235-6468-1

Series: Bloomsbury Adaptation Histories

Typeset by Integra Software Services Pvt. Ltd.
Printed and bound in the United States of America

Contents

List of Figures

Acknowledgements

I am deeply indebted to Katie Gallof and Mary Al-Sayed at Bloomsbury Academic for their generosity and patience. I am grateful to Imelda Whelehan for her, as usual, extremely helpful advice and to Ian, Jake and Hester Bradley for their support.

Finally, many thanks to the British Film Institute's Reuben Library for the use of their magnificent collection of pressbooks.

Introduction: 'Singin' in the Rain': Adapting Literature to Film, 1927–37

For better or worse, adaptation studies (not to be confused with film adaptations themselves) begins with the 'all talking' adaptation. The first decade of sound cinema is a defining period for film adaptations of literary and dramatic texts, particularly 'classic' texts. Through considering the nature of film adaptations in the first decade of sound, I argue that it is apparent that the introduction of sound, or spoken words, transformed how an adaptation, in particular, a film adaptation of a well-known literary work, was defined. The advent of sound, ultimately, did no favours for the field of adaptation studies. Due to the presence of spoken words, the unprofitable approach of comparing the words of a book to those spoken in a film (what has become known as the 'fidelity approach' in the field of adaptation studies) begins in earnest in the advertising campaigns promoting the talkie film adaptations as the *first ever* adaptations of an author's works. During the first ten years of sound cinema, 'classic' film adaptations' valuation in relation to words, and reputation as inoffensive, wholesome and conservative evolved, a reputation that has done much to stigmatize these films as well as accounting for their uncertain place within film and literary studies.

Twenty-first century writers on adaptation have, more often than not, approached adaptation studies (in particular screen adaptations of literary texts) by reflecting on what is wrong with the field. The most vociferous of these complaints are: it is battling against a no-win mindset that a film has to be 'faithful' to the book it claims to be based upon;[1] its approach is often

---

[1] Robert Stam, 'The Aporias of "Fidelity"', 'Introduction', in *Literature and Film: A Guide to the Theory and Practice of Film Adaptation*, ed. Robert. Stam and Alessandra Raengo (Malden: Blackwell, 2003), 14–16.

oblivious to the economic and industrial factors shaping the end product;[2] it disregards the screenplay, costumes, soundtrack, casting and other aspects of the production;[3] its boundaries are becoming too wide;[4] and it relies too heavily on the 'case study'. Critics have tended to approach adaptations via literary texts (for instance, a study of a single text of Shakespeare or Austen) or genre (for instance looking at the development of Gothic or Science Fiction adaptations) rather than situating them within a specific historical context. James Naremore, writing at the turn of the twentieth/twenty-first centuries, echoing some of the concerns of the cultural materialist critics of Shakepeare,[5] suggests that adaptation scholars 'ask why certain canonical books have been of interest to Hollywood' and 'what conditions of the marketplace govern the desire for textual fidelity.'[6] This book (and the series as a whole) attempts to answer such questions and aims to consider film adaptations as products of and responding to issues and debates of specific historical periods, reading adaptations in relation to other adaptations produced within the same period, rather than reading films based on the same 'source' text, the same director or the same genre.

Adaptation studies has tended to consider novels and plays, on the whole, in relation to each other rather than with regard to others produced at the same time. Even in the most insightful analyses, such as Thomas Leitch's *Film Adaptation and Its Discontents: From 'Gone with the Wind' to*

---

[2] See, for instance, Simone Murray, 'A principal, but little-acknowledged, cost of this near-exclusive attention to "what" has been adapted across media has been an understanding of "how" adaptation functions industrially: namely, the stakeholders, institutions, commercial arrangements and legal frameworks which govern the flow of content across media', 'Phantom adaptations: *Eucalyptus*, the adaptation industry and the film that never was', *Adaptation* 1(1) (2008), 5–23.

[3] For example, Jack Boozer laments the lack of attention given to the screenplay in his 'Introduction', in *Authorship in Film Adaptation*, ed. Jack Boozer (Austin: University of Texas Press, 2008), 1–30.

[4] Thomas Leitch surveys attempts to define what constitutes an adaptation in 'Adaptation and Intertextuality, or What isn't an Adaptation, and What Does it Matter', in *A Companion to Literature, Film and Adaptation*, ed. Deborah Cartmell (Oxford: Blackwell 2012), 87–104.

[5] See for instance, *Political Shakespeare: Essays in Cultural Materialism*, ed. Jonathan Dollimore and Alan Sinfield, 1985, 2nd ed. (Manchester: Manchester University Press, 1996); *The Shakespeare Myth*, ed. Graham Holderness (Manchester: Manchester University Press, 1988).

[6] James Naremore, 'Introduction', in *Film Adaptation*, ed. James Naremore (New Jersey: Rutgers University Press, 2000), 11.

'*The Passion of the Christ*' (2007), film versions of a single text, such as *A Christmas Carol*, are read through a dizzying array of *Christmas Carols*, from the silent period to the present day, implicitly assuming that the single text binds them together in a virtually ahistorical world.[7] So, rather than look at a film adaptation of *David Copperfield* in relation to the production values and competition of a given time, scholars in the field seem to prefer to look at a novel and a film in isolation or longitudinally in relation to a trajectory of *David Copperfield*s, considering how the novel has changed over time and regarding the films in some kind of dialogue with an urtext. This series, and this book, aim to look at adaptations from an historical perspective: why texts were chosen, how adaptations were marketed, what formula worked, what failed, how literary texts are promoted and disguised in films of a given period and how these film adaptations respond to each other.

This book considers adaptations in the period of sound, from 1927 to 1937, and argues that adaptation studies, as we have come to loathe it ('the not as good as the book approach'), developed alongside the introduction of sound when the words spoken become of paramount importance when a canonical text, in particular, is adapted. Much of the research for the book is taken from marketing materials and reviews that help us gauge the perceived audience of the talkie adaptation. Because the spoken words, that is how many words were retained and how they were pronounced, were perceived of as increasingly important in respect of the value of the adapted text, this book will focus on a range of adaptations, from Shakespeare to more popular writers, to adaptations which in their promotional materials and the presentation of the texts within the films, revere the adapted author to those in which the author is of little or no importance. Adaptations, of this period, will be read through the ways in which the films position themselves as adaptations, more often than not in opposition to the ways in which they

---

[7] Thomas Leitch discusses 'Entry-Level Dickens', *A Christmas Carol* adaptations as designed to 'convert' audiences, in particular children to Dickens in *Film Adaptation and Its Discontents: From 'Gone with the Wind' to 'The Passion of the Christ'* (Baltimore: Johns Hopkins University Press, 2007), 67–92 . The chapter ranges from adaptations in the silent period to more recent films, reflecting on the persistence of this story on screen.

were advertised to the public.[8] It tries to do more and less than Guerric DeBona's *Film Adaptation in the Hollywood Studio Era* (2010) in that it will look at considerably more films than those covered by DeBona (one film in this period, MGM's 1935 *David Copperfield*, is given extensive coverage) and within a shorter time period (1927–37 rather than 1935–51).[9]

Adaptation criticism, sound and theatre

Adaptation critics often cite George Bluestone's *Novels into Film* (1958) as the first full-length study of adaptations. However, the first monograph on the subject is more than twenty years earlier, Allardyce Nicoll's *Film and Theatre*, published in 1936, a book, which like this study, takes stock of the sound film and the hybrid form which it creates. While Nicoll champions the sound film, arguing for restraint in the use of dialogue, he regrets its reliance on intertitles within a film, citing Jack Conway's *A Tale of Two Cities* (1936) as a prime example of this regressive tendency.[10] Nicoll also argues against fidelity, again citing *A Tale of Two Cities*: 'simply to follow the plan of a novel in the preparing of a screen-play is a procedure as erroneous as the faithful reproduction of the screen of dramatic form.'[11] The author of this wide-ranging and forward-thinking book calls attention to the intermingling of novel and theatrical genres, insofar as novel adaptations are more often than not mediated through theatre (the 'source' text being an adapted play of a novel) and as films, the 'novel adaptations' are themselves, often regarded and dismissed as unnecessarily theatrical.

---

[8] Julie Sanders in *Adaptation and Appropriation* defines adaptation (as opposed to appropriation) as a text that positions itself as such (Abingdon and New York: Routledge, 2006). But it is worth bearing in mind that we cannot assume intentionality as Thomas Leitch reminds us. However, he does agree that 'A definition of adaptation that emphasizes intentionality and reception is fundamentally economic because it inevitably focuses on the motives and interests that provide legal, moral, and aesthetic sanction for some kinds of copies, the derivations that are not derivative, but not others. Instead of seeking the scientific neutrality of terms like 'intermediality', this model accepts the metaphorical baggage that comes with the term 'adaptation' as a problem to be addressed head-on.' 'Adaptation and Intertextuality, or What isn't an Adaptation, and What Does it Matter?', 96.

[9] *Film Adaptation in the Hollywood Studio Era* (Urbana, Chicago and Springfield: University of Illinois Press, 2010).

[10] *Film and Theatre* (London: George G. Harrap, 1936), 146–7.

[11] *Theatre and Film*, 160.

What we tend to forget when viewing these films today is that the original audiences and filmmakers in the late 1920s and early 1930s were, as Nicoll, writing in the mid 1930s, reminds us, both sceptical and in awe of sound; and the self-conscious use of sound, in particular the spoken word, needs to be taken into consideration in any analysis of these films as adaptations. Adaptations chosen for this book are largely those that were commissioned by the major Hollywood studios for their prestige and commercial value and include adaptations of Shakespeare, Dickens, gothic fiction, biographies and children's literature, each of which has to appeal to the masses as well as setting themselves up to the mockery of the disbelievers, among them literary critics, historians and educationalists. The fear that a film could replace the book, or that the existence of the adaptation would be a threat to the reading of the novel or play, potentially obliterating historical evidence and literary value, had never been stronger. The obsessive campaigns recommended in the pressbooks released in this period, to involve schools, reading groups, bookshops, universities, women's clubs, church groups and academics, are strong evidence of a major concern that these adaptations were perceived by many as a threat to the predominance of the written word and to historical fidelity.

The voice

It is well known that from 1927, after the release of *The Jazz Singer*, the first major feature-length picture with sound, the major Hollywood studios (led by Warner Brothers) converted silent cinema to cinema with sound, with actors who could talk (many imported from the stage), making their film debuts and old film actors who could not or would not talk taking their bows. Maurice Chevalier, Edward G. Robinson and Katherine Hepburn, emerged in this period, all of whom had distinctive voices, while actors like John Gilbert, who rivalled Rudolph Valentino in the silent period, were ejected from the limelight. Although now disputed, it was claimed that Gilbert's voice let him down. Greta Garbo survived (her first talkie, *Anna Christie*, 1930, was fuelled with publicity regarding the actress's voice: 'GRETA GARBO TALKS!'). But Mary Pickford, sweetheart of the silent screen, retired from acting in 1933, as the demands of the new talkie proved a bridge too far. Advice on elocution was everywhere at the beginning of the sound period. James R. Quirk, writing in the September, 1929 issue of *Photoplay* offers some words of wisdom: 'THOSE stars who have been spending money on lessons in high tea English had better return to their original Kansas accents. Phony English accents – learned in ten sessions with an elocution teacher – aren't going, so big with audiences.' He reminds his readers that while 'A GENUINE English accent, spoken by a British born actor or actress, stirs up no resentment' 'our won American language, clearly pronounced and intelligently spoken, is better than the messy English accent so much affected by third-rate stock company players.'[12] In December of the same year, *Photoplay* ran an article entitled 'The Microphone – The Terror of the Studios' with a devil descending from the sky wielding a microphone, causing stars to flee in terror[13] (See Figure 1.1).

Hollywood producers in this period turned to the theatre and hired theatrical professionals: actors, directors, writers and composers. The April issue of *Photoplay*'s cover asked 'Are the Stage Actors Stealing the Screen?'[14] The answer, it seemed, was a resounding 'yes' in the early days of sound cinema.

The conversion to sound

In the midst of the Depression, equipping the studios and theatres to sound was a costly enterprise, but one which paid dividends for the new talkie. This is a highly simplified interpretation of the conversion to sound, one that is perhaps too influenced by the myth of the transformation from silence to sound as narrated in *Singin' in the Rain* (1952). Such a view, popularized by *Singin' in the Rain*, about the transition from Old to New Hollywood is one that needs to be tempered. As Donald Crafton writes, Hollywood adapted to sound, not in an overnight conversion, but in a more measured and systematic fashion:

---

[12] https://archive.org/stream/photoplay3637movi#page/n323/mode/2up, accessed 6 March 2014.
[13] https://archive.org/stream/photoplay3637movi#page/28/mode/2up, accessed 6 March 2014.
[14] https://archive.org/stream/photoplay3738movi#page/n429/mode/2up, accessed 6 March 2014.

The Microphone–*The Terror*

Of The Studios   By Harry Lang

Mike, the demon, who sends the vocally unfit screaming or lisping from the lots

THIS is a story of Terrible Mike, the capricious genie of Hollywood, who is a Pain in the Larynx to half of filmdom, and a Tin Santa Claus to the other half!—who gives a Yoo-Hoo-There Leading Man a Voice like a Bull, and makes a Cauliflower-Eared Heavy talk like Elfin Elbert, the Library Lizard!—and who has raised more hell in movieland than a clara bow in a theological seminary.

Why, you can't even begin to write the half of the story of Terrible Mike and what he's done. You can only take a heap of ha-ha's here, and boo-hoo's there—laughs and sobs, heart-leaps and heart-aches, sudden wealth and sudden ruin, funny things and tragic things and howcum things—and try to string 'em together into some semblance of yarn.

And even then, every Hector' and Hectorine that struts the streets of Hollywood will read it and say: "This guy ain't said NAW-thin' yet. . . ." And they'll be right—but here goes.

* * *

IN the first place—or is it? but let's put it there—young John W. Microphone, to give Terrible Mike his family name, has made the leading lady of the screen a LADY in fact as well as in name. Not that she wasn't ALWAYS a lady—no one'd EVER go so far as to say that. But look— Before Mike crashed the studio gate and brought in his lady friends, what was little Miss Starlet like? You know. Ya-da-da-DA-poo-POO;—let's GO!!!—THAT'S what she was.

29

Figure 1.1 *Photoplay*, December 1929, p. 28

The industry responded according to a classic paradigm consisting of three phases. 'Invention' covers the development of the synch-sound apparatus up to 1925 when Warner Bros became interested in exploiting it as Vitaphone. 'Innovation' includes the period when Vitaphone, Fox and the 'Big Five' studios defined various ways of applying sound. This phase ended in 1928 when the majors decided together to commit themselves to sound. 'Diffusion' was the coordinated dissemination of sound domestically and abroad according to mutually beneficial terms dictated by the studios. This phase also included the swift wiring of theatres.[15]

As Crafton points out, Warner Brothers' *The Jazz Singer* did not convince the other companies to immediately cease the production of silent films, but it did persuade them of the potential of star voices and popular music in films. Before *The Jazz Singer*, sound film was largely about music with the initial Vitaphone concept of replacing expensive orchestras with recorded tracks. Talking film was a more expensive and risky venture. Many who were closely involved in film were opposed to the talkie, regarding it as a flash in the pan. Thomas Edison, while believing in the technology, felt that it would never catch on.[16] The editor of the *Film Spectator* in the same year saw the talking picture and the idea of television as toys, to be played with for a while, but ultimately discarded: 'We stood for the phonograph and the radio, but talking pictures carry the thing just a little too far.'[17] Certainly, in the early years of sound film, the jury was very much out as to whether sound film would replace silent cinema. According to Donald Crafton, 1928–29 was the year of the 'big hedge': 'some of these films talked, some did not, and some looked just like the slapped-together concoctions they were. Several directors tried on sound in various sizes and shapes, looking for a crowd-pleasing fit. Meanwhile, consumers were also exposed to considerable marketing hype about the talkies'.[18] By 1930, concerns about the influence of the talkies were voiced in *Photoplay*: 'THE only universal language ever known was the silent picture. The talkies have re-created the

---

[15] Donald Crafton, *The Talkies: American Cinema's Transition to Sound: 1926–1931* (Berkeley: University of California Press, 1999), 3–4.
[16] 4 March 1927, 1, 2, quoted in Crafton, 101.
[17] 21 September 1929, 140, quoted in Crafton, 27.
[18] Crafton, 311.

Tower of Babel. They have also re-awakened consciousness of nationality in a manner that can be equaled only by a war.'[19]

The promotion of sound

Promoters of films in the early sound era wholly ignored the sound sceptics and worked to perpetuate the notion of a new era of film, frequently stressing the revolutionary nature and the benefits of the new technology in their publicity materials. Technology itself became a major selling point. An advertisement for Western Electric Sound System in *Photoplay* in June 1930 proclaimed 'Which theatre to-night? Let the EAR TEST decide . . . . Find out which houses in your neighborhood are using Western Electric equipment – look for the identifying sign in the lobby.'[20]

The promotional literature surrounding film adaptations of novels and plays focused on the possibilities offered by the new technology. Sound allowed adaptations to be more 'faithful' to their literary narratives than ever before in that the author's words were no longer abbreviated and reproduced to be read, but to be spoken. How they were spoken and how many of the words were retained became important selling points, implicitly, praising the new cinema's reliance on theatre. As Nicoll reminds us, a remarkable number of the films of this period come to the screen through plays and adaptations in the theatre. For instance, *The Doctor's Secret* (1929) was a Paramount's adaptation of J.M. Barrie's play, *Half an Hour*, MGM's *The Trial of Mary Dugan* (1929) was an adaption of a Broadway production, Tod Browning's *Dracula* was developed from the 1924 stage play by Hamilton Deane and John L. Balderston, James Whale's *Frankenstein* was based on the 1927 adaptation by Peggy Webling and Rouben Mamoulian's 1931 *Dr. Jekyll and Mr. Hyde* stems from the Thomas Russell Sullivan play of 1887. The emphasis on theatrical performance (in spite of this also being the case in many silent films) and the corresponding

---

[19] James R. Quirk, *Photoplay*, November, 1930, https://archive.org/stream/photoplay3839movi#page/n633/mode/2up, accessed 6 March 2014.

[20] *Photoplay*, June 1930, https://archive.org/stream/photoplay3738movi#page/110/mode/2up, accessed 6 March 2014.

impression of 'filmed theatre' (partially due to the location of the microphone, rendering an overall static presentation), however, served to devalue the films in the minds of film critics (and to a certain extent, persists today) insofar as the adaptations tended to be appreciated for their theatrical rather than their cinematic qualities. The excessive theatricality of the new talkie led George Bernard Shaw to predict the demise of theatre itself: 'THE poor old theater is done for, I'm afraid. All my plays will be done into talkies before long. What other course is open to me? The theater may survive as a place where people are taught to act. Apart from that, there will be nothing but talkies soon.'[21]

Adaptations in the first decade of sound: radical beginnings, conservative endings

The Oscars for best film in the 1930s were dominated by adaptations of novels or of historical figures, revealing an appetite for cinematic recreations of literary and historical narratives, perhaps because the stories filmed had been demonstrated to be both safe and/or commercially viable. Academy award winners include *All Quiet on the Western Front* (adapted from the 1929 novel by Erich Maria Remarque), *Cimmarron* (adapted from the 1929 novel by Edna Ferber), *Grand Hotel* (based on a 1930 play by William A. Drake, which was an adaptation of 1929 novel *Menschen im Hotel* by Vicki Baum), *Calvacade* (the film version of Noël Coward's 1931 play), *It Happened One Night* (an adaptation of a 1933 short story, 'Night Bus' by Samuel Hopkins Adams), *Mutiny on the Bounty* based on Charles Nordhoff and James Norman Hall's *Mutiny on the Bounty* of 1932, *The Great Ziegfeld*, *The Life of Emile Zola* and *You Can't Take It With You* (based on a 1936 play by George S. Kaufman and Moss Hart).

Adaptations attracted big stars and expected big audiences. With the exception of the Oscar winning 1930 film, *All Quiet on the Western Front*, directed by Lewis Milestone and adapted by George Abbott, Maxwell Anderson and Del Andrews, these adaptations seem to retreat from overt

---

[21] Quoted in *Photoplay*, 'Talking of Talkies', November, 1930, https://archive.org/stream/photoplay 3839movi#page/n739/mode/2up, accessed 6 March 2014.

engagement with political and social issues of the period with a seeming aim to be as unobjectionable as possible. Made in both silent and sound versions, *All Quiet on the Western Front* focuses on German soldiers and the suffering they needlessly endured during the First World War. Mordaunt Hall's *New York Times* review of 1930 encapsulates the immediate effect the film had on its original audience, many of whom would have experienced the war first-hand: 'Carl Laemmle's Universal Pictures Corporation has produced a trenchant and imaginative audible picture, in which the producers adhere with remarkable fidelity to the spirit and events of the original stirring novel. It was presented last night at the Central Theatre before an audience that most of the time was held to silence by its realistic scenes. It is a notable achievement, sincere and earnest, with glimpses that are vivid and graphic. Like the original, it does not mince matters concerning the horrors of battle. It is a vocalized screen offering that is pulsating and harrowing, one in which the fighting flashes are photographed in an amazingly effective fashion.'[22] The (for Hall) exceptionally long review conveys a sense of astonishment in what the film was able to achieve. Even by today's standards the film is shocking in its relentless focus on the horrors of war from the perspective of the young German soldiers (played by American actors, which brings the enemies together in a common humanity). The sounds of gunfire and explosions dominate the film. At the end of the movie, when the protagonist's hand is seen reaching out to capture a butterfly, we hear the final gun shot and see the hand in suspended motion. With this image, silence, after so much noise, shockingly descends. The final frames of the film reinforce the message of war's circularity with the young soldiers as seen at the beginning of the movie, marching purposefully to war while each looks wistfully backwards, this time superimposed with a field of white crosses. Widely admired, the film was the first talkie to win an Academy Award. Although heavily censored, it was even praised by the Motion Picture Producers and Distributors of America (albeit with substantial cuts) as 'A very faithful adaptation .... The spirit of the book has been exceedingly well portrayed'.[23] Expressed here is a 'belief' in the

---

[22] Mordaunt Hall, April 30, 1930, http://www.nytimes.com/movie/review?res=980DE7D81738E03AB C4850DFB266838B629EDE, accessed 20 July 2014.

[23] This is the report of an officer of the MPPDA at première of the film. See Andrew Kelly, '*All Quiet on the Western Front': The Story of a Film* (London: I.B. Tauris, 1998), 107.

moral value of literature of quality and that if the adaptation is 'faithful' then it should be agreeable to the censors. However, the film was so heavily cut, from country to country, that after the initial course of the film, there was not a surviving full print of the movie. The film's reception in Germany was on a wholly different scale. Due to the demythologizing of the war, in particular the depictions of the German soldiers as traumatized victims, Joseph Goebbels orchestrated riots at the film's German première, with protesters shouting 'Judenfilm'. Six days after the première in Germany, the German Supreme Film Censorship Board officially banned the film.[24]

Such an overtly socially and politically charged adaptation was not to be repeated in the early sound period. The desire for commercial success overrules scruples as Thomas Doherty notes; in order to maintain a German audience, Jewish characters were pushed aside (in spite of the fact that the studios were overseen by Jewish moguls and that there was a huge influx into Hollywood of German artists, especially Jews fleeing from the Nazi regime) in order to gain the approval of the German censors. From 1933, Joseph Goebbels ensured that, as Thomas Doherty observes, 'the elimination of Jews from the German film industry was sudden, ruthless and comprehensive',[25] a policy that extended to imports from Hollywood. Max Reinhardt's *A Midsummer Night's Dream* of 1935, for example, was banned in Germany a year before its release due to the Jewish backgrounds of Reinhardt and composer Felix Mendelssohn.[26] The Motion Picture Production Code, also known as the Hays Code after its main censor, Will H. Hays, provides a reason for the choice of adaptations in Hollywood during this period. Introduced in 1930 and rigorously enforced in 1934, it regulated against the likes of profanity, nudity, miscegenation and offence to any nation or creed. The left-wing journal, *New Theatre and Film*, saw such censorship – or 'purification' – in league with a Nazi threat, pointing out a German film journal referring to 'Kardinal Hayes, the führer of the well-known clean film movement in the USA.'[27]

---

[24] For a discussion of the cuts, country by country, see Ibid.

[25] Thomas Doherty, *Hollywood and Hitler: 1933-1939* (New York: Columbia Press, 2013), 21.

[26] Doherty, 26.

[27] Carl Dreher, 'Parade-Ground Art: The German Film under Hitler', in *New Theatre and Film: 1934–1937*, ed. Herbert Kline (San Diego: Harcourt Brace, 1985), 327–337, 329.

Responding to demands for wholesome entertainment, the edifying and morally uplifting nature of adaptations of canonical literature is reiterated throughout the pressbooks. The selling points of these films are neatly summed up in the pressbook to the 1933 *Little Women*: 'THE STAR, THE STORY, THE SCHOOLS'.[28] The distinctive feature of these films is 'THE SCHOOLS', that is their alleged educational value. Suggestions for marketing the 1933 *Alice in Wonderland*, for instance, include 'FREE SHOWINGS FOR KIDS, ORPHANS, NEWSBOYS ETC' and 'SCHOOLS ARE "NATURALS" FOR "ALICE"'.[29] The family attraction of the film is also not missed in these marketing ploys: 'CHRISTMAS and ' "Alice" go' hand in hand'.[30] Indeed, many of the adaptations, such as *Little Women* and the many Dickens adaptations of this period, draw on Christmas celebrations and music, reinforcing a sense of a unified community and Christian values, seemingly oblivious to developments in Germany or to the Jewish backgrounds of those involved in their production.

The period of the talkie is normally considered to span 1927–31 after which the term 'talkie' was no longer descriptive, as it was applicable to all films. The early sound films up until 1929 were often merely vehicles to show off the sound effects, while during 1929–30, musicals became a dominant product of the big studios. Reacting to a perceived overdose of sound, due the musicals of 1929–30, the films of 1930–31 were much quieter, on the whole. Nonetheless, a taste for adaptations of novels and short magazine stories was on the rise.[31] Concerns regarding the voice and the need for elocution training had vanished by 1929 when unusual voices and accents were actively encouraged. But the introduction of spoken words brought a new layer of censorship and in 1930, the Production Code was revised with the impact of sound in mind.[32]

Nonetheless, the novelty of sound persisted well into the 1930s with moviegoers unlikely to entirely forget the recent silent past. This book aims to look at a selection of adaptations in the sound era in their capacity as

---

[28] *Little Women*, Pressbook, 1933.
[29] *Alice in Wonderland*, Pressbook, 1933, 12.
[30] Pressbook, 12.
[31] Crafton, 380.
[32] Crafton, 474.

adaptations, paying particular attention to the novelty of the spoken word and the marketing and reception of these films. In spite of the fact that many of these adaptations, such as *Jekyll and Hyde* (1931) are, in part, adaptations of an earlier silent film, the marketing of these films, on the whole, proclaims them to be 'firsts', definitive versions (with no expectation of a remake). The implication is that a film adaptation of a literary work is only possible if the words are retained and spoken: the quest for fidelity in advertising and in critiquing these films begins in earnest in the sound era. But the adaptations themselves often tell a very different story.

Considered among the most enduring film adaptations released in this period are *All Quiet on the Western Front* (1930), *Dracula* (1931), *Frankenstein* (1931), *Dr. Jekyll and Mr. Hyde* (1931), *Little Women* (1933), *Alice in Wonderland* (1933), *The Bride of Frankenstein* (1935), *A Tale of Two Cities* (1935), *Mutiny on the Bounty* (1935), *Heidi* (1937) and *Snow White and the Seven Dwarfs* (1937).[33] Many of these films qualify as 'prestige pictures' based on literature, history or biography, films which the industry staked its reputation on and which sought critical as much as commercial success. This book aims to range across different types of adaptation, from those that fall into the prestige category to those that were made for commercial rather than 'artistic' motives.

The use of an author's words and the moral or edifying nature of these films come to define them as adaptations in this period, with the films presenting themselves, in spite of their silent predecessors, as the first adaptation of an author's work. This perception of silent adaptations as 'non-adaptation' has prevailed for most of the post-sound period and can be felt in what we now refer to as 'fidelity criticism', judging a film's value in relation to its closeness to the literary text it apes.

As I have indicated, adaptation criticism, defined as a means of popularizing literature by introducing a novel or play through a 'more accessible' film, was invented in the early sound era, a period in which words, especially of a canonical author, carry a new weight. The introduction of sound initiated the first phase of adaptation studies, emerging through the

---

[33] http://www.imdb.com/search/title?at=0&release_date=1930,1939&sort=moviemeter,asc&start=10 1&title_type=feature. From the IMDB top 100 list, accessed April 11, 2014.

promotional materials these films generated which perpetuated the myth that words were the single most important feature of an adaptation.

Literary opposition

There is a significant silence regarding film adaptations in literary criticism of this period and while it is entirely possible to avoid seeing the films, it would have been virtually impossible to escape the extensive marketing of these movies. F.R. Leavis, hardly a film fan, writing in this same period, identified advertising as the lowest and most insidious form of writing in its blatant underhanded methods and shameless materialism. Nonetheless, he put it to use to expose the tackiness of writers who aimed to be 'popular', or middle-brow as opposed to high-brow, sneering, like many of his contemporaries, at popular culture. In *Mass Civilisation and Minority Culture* (1930), he attacks writers like Hugh Walpole and Arnold Bennett for stooping to the tactics of advertisers who unapologetically appeal to the lowest possible denominator in order to attract the widest audiences. Leavis's unwitting legacy to adaptation studies can be traced to *Mass Civilisation and Minority Culture* (1930) and with Denys Thompson, *Culture and Environment* (1933): both books teach (or warn against) the menace of popularization. The concerns expressed within these two books, among them anxieties regarding the decay of language, the standardization of literary texts and the distrust for new technologies can be considered within the context of the rise of the talkie adaptation (from 1927 onwards) and the marketing of film adaptations in the 1930s.

In *Mass Civilisation*, Leavis moves from discussing the defects of popular writing to the even worse example of film and then focuses on advertising, to demonstrate the inferiority of these forms that use 'cheap tricks' to attract an audience. For Leavis, the popular novel descends into the cheap thrills of cinema, which in turn descends into advertising which appeals to the base appetite rather than the rational faculties. English academics have been historically uncomfortable with literature that has a popular appeal and this is an integral part of Leavis's legacy to the teaching of literature and to the formation of the English canon for most of the twentieth century. The belief that if a book is favoured by a mass audience, then it must not be good, became largely unspoken but deep-rooted in English literature departments and within the culture of English education in general, perhaps because of what Leavis would see as popular literature's unholy alliance with advertising. What defines popular writing and, even more so, film, for Leavis, is its commerciality or its unacknowledged dependence on the tactics of advertising, a dependence that Leavis and his colleagues, among them Q.D. Leavis and Denys Thompson, were determined to expose. Significantly, these critics wilfully linked popular literature, cinema and advertising in their writing. Q.D. Leavis, for instance, sees the commercial targeting of the audience rather than appealing to the author's own inclinations as the root of the problem: she writes in *Fiction and the Reading Public* (1932) that 'fear of the herd, approval of the herd, the peace of mind that comes from conforming with the herd, are the strings they play upon and the ideals that inform [the popular author's] work'.[34] The same could be said of cinema.

Even more than Q.D. Leavis, Leavis himself did not ignore advertising as something unworthy of mention, but tackled it head on. For Leavis and Thompson, teaching English was not a far cry, peculiarly, to teaching advertising, or to unpacking the strategically hidden messages embedded within writing specifically designed to promote a product. In *Culture and Environment*, the need to teach or expose what lies behind advertising is outlined. Leavis and Thompson make it their mission to teach the hidden tactics employed by advertisers, designed to darken the minds of thousands at the cost of enlightenment, to offer what they called 'substitute living' at the expense of the appreciation of high culture.

Leavis and Thompson begin their book with the question about the value of English teaching: 'What effect can such training have against the multitudinous counter-influences – films, newspapers, advertising – indeed, the whole world outside the classroom?'[35] The language used to sell these inferior products is scrutinized in *Culture and Environment* by bringing it

---

[34] Q.D. Leavis, *Fiction and the Reading Public* (1932; rpt. London: Random House, 2000),192.

[35] F.R. Leavis and Denys Thompson, *Culture and Environment* (London: Chatto & Windus, 1933), 1.

to the classroom, and ninety-three specimen exercises for sixth form classes were included at the end of the book. The authors draw heavily on Jan and Cora Gordon's *Star-Dust in Hollywood*, an exposé of Hollywood in the late 1920s which ends with 'the madness of the movietone' which at the time of writing was shockingly going to cost 'as high as a dollar for every word spoken'.[36] The equation of words with money, writing and commerce was clearly the last straw in this book and one that would clearly strike a chord with the Leavis circle. That Leavis and Thompson are writing *Culture and Environment* with a copy of *Star-Dust in Hollywood* to hand is revealing of the motivations underlying their enterprise.

As Christopher Hilliard argues in his study of the *Scrutiny* Movement, Leavis's teaching was animated by a belief that 'a literary training armed to resist the intellectually deadening and emotionally limiting tendencies of mass culture' was seen as most necessary.[37] Analogous to the critique of the effects of the Industrial Revolution on the nineteenth century, advertising, journalism, film and best selling fiction were drivers of modern civilization, a threat to the appreciation of the 'higher' forms of culture. Film and in particular, the talkie, or even worse, the talkie adaptation, were calamitous desecrators of language and, therefore, of culture itself. But Leavis, like Machiavelli, was keen that we should know the enemy; and that good students should be taught to understand how the destroyers of culture operate so that they could join the cultural minority and abstain.

These writings of Leavis and his contemporary literary critics were produced in the early 1930s, in the new era of the talking film, which indirectly posed an even stronger threat to those teaching 'English literature' insofar as the films were now employing actual speaking words 'stolen' from the classics. The advertisers were becoming literary critics themselves, employing the services of so-called academics to make claims for the literary value of film adaptations. Leavis has a lot to say about advertising, something to say about film but hardly anything to say about film adaptation and we can interpret

---

[36] Jan Gordon and Cora Gordon, *Star-Dust in Hollywood* (London: George G. Harrap & Co., 1930), 281.

[37] Christopher Hilliard, *English as a Vocation: The Scrutiny Movement* (Oxford: Oxford University Press, 2012), 37.

this silence as reflecting an anxiety about the threat posed by film adaptation which, as I have argued, was decidedly banished from *Scrutiny* from the first issue onwards.[38] E.S. Turner has demonstrated how the debunking of advertising was popular on both sides of the Atlantic in the early 1930s and the most exploitative advertising was the advertising of film; 'No industry did more to destroy the meaning of words.'[39] Turner explains how cinema managers 'were deluged' with

> … 'campaign sheets' full of brash ideas for engineering local publicity and 'tie-ups'. Any manager who carried out one tenth of these suggestions was well on the way to becoming the most unpopular man in his community. He was urged to suborn local clergymen, Army officers and heads of stores to help publicize his attractions; he was told to invite senior pupils from schools to see films about adultery; he was prodded to promote kissing contests and leg competitions, to hire hunchbacks.[40]

From the advertiser's perspective, the talking picture placed the adaptation in a different light – it was now, as its promoters joyfully proclaimed, even closer to its literary source, so much so that, as noted above, advertisers were claiming these were the first adaptations of an author's work, in spite of numerous silent precursors and that the adaptations could indeed better their literary predecessors.[41]

Much to the disgust of literary critics and 'high brow' writers, advertisers of these first talkies repeatedly boasted these films' fidelity to their literary sources; so insistently and powerfully were these arguments made that they became the yardstick to measure an adaptation's merit, a measure which persisted, infuriatingly for adaptation champions, for most of the remaining twentieth century. Promoters of these early talkie adaptations of texts such as those by Shakespeare, Dickens and other adaptations produce an early version of adaptation studies, with suggestions as to how to consume the films as pedagogical tools, inviting exhibitors to offer them up to school children as entrances to the great works of literature. The pressbooks provide the first

---

[38] See discussion of *The Taming of the Shrew*, 1929, in the following chapter.
[39] A.S. Turner, *The Shocking History of Advertising* (London: Penguin, 1952), 209.
[40] Turner, 210.
[41] See Chapter 2 and the discussion of *The Taming of the Shrew*'s promotional materials.

forays into the field of adaptations, often with the message that the film will help audiences understand the book, bringing it 'alive'.

These pressbooks of early talkie adaptations offer an early form of adaptation studies, through the obsessive marketing of the cultural capital these films provide. The pressbook for *As You Like It* (1936), for instance regards the film as 'explaining' the play and issued a 'Study Guide' which as its publisher's name, 'Educational and Recreational Guides' states, mixes work with pleasure. Thousands of sample copies have been mailed to high schools, educators and clubs throughout the United States.'[42] This guide, in particular, combines an understanding of the film with an analysis of the play: 'Through information, photographs and questions, the student is enabled to analyse the entire production. Fascinating technical points in the production of the film are made and sections are devoted to the study of dramatic values, the characters and Shakespeare.'[43] The film is marketed for its educational value, for sweetening the harshness of Shakespeare, for making Shakespeare fun: 'So you *think* you don't like Shakespeare? There's a surprise for all you folks!'[44] Adaptation studies, although it did not exist as such, took the form of serving to lighten the literary source in an alleged effort to convert filmgoers to literature. The appeal was not to those who knew the plays but to those who did not. This approach would feed into the worst fears of those enemies of adaptation who could not help but worry that the prevailing attitude would be why read a book when you can see the film?

Leavis and Thompson were keen to teach the evils of advertising, to alert students to the seductive powers that pull the audience down to the lowest possible denominator. However, Christopher Hilliard argues that Leavis was in part bizarrely responsible for the rise of Media Studies through his opening up of texts of advertising and popular fiction.[45] In fact, Leavis and Thompson's work on advertising and literature offers an (albeit) unwitting model for an approach to adaptations which to date has paid scant attention

---

[42] *As You Like It*, Pressbook, 1936.
[43] Ibid.
[44] Ibid.
[45] 'The *Scrutiny* movement's work on the subject was the foundation of media studies in Britain and part of the patrimony of several generations of teachers and students, many of whom took positions on mass culture and modernity sharply different from those of Leavis and Thompson.' (48).

to the commercial paratexts which surround it. Adaptation studies, as Simone Murray has reminded us, should be about the marketability of the entertainment that strategically positions the consumer as the primary target. Murray calls attention to a significant blind spot in the field that has, until recently, refused to take account of 'the stakeholders, institutions, commercial arrangements and legal frameworks which govern the flow of the content across media'.[46] Rather than conceal its industrial and commercial motivations, the field should seek to uncover and unpack these.

Conclusions

This book groups adaptations chronologically by genre and author (an expedient, if somewhat problematic approach that admittedly presupposes the existence of generic communities of movies, imposed on the films perhaps more by their critics than by their own design). The study focuses on a ten-year period, assessing the rise of the talkie adaptation in its many incarnations: Shakespeare films which failed to impress audiences or achieve the anticipated kudos for the studios, Dickens adaptations which found both popularity and acclaim (a success that was repeated in later years with newer adaptations overshadowing and virtually obliterating the pioneering films of the 1930s), Gothic adaptations which, against all the odds, became classics perhaps due to their downplaying of the literary texts, biopics, or adaptations of historical figures that strive for visual verisimilitude with little regard for the subjects' words and children's adaptations which in their promotional materials overtly attempt to assuage concerns regarding film's morality and the perceived threat to literacy. It is abundantly clear from the promotional materials that these films were aiming to appeal to as wide an audience as possible, what Leavis describes as 'mass civilisation'. Emerging in this period is a covert battle between the film promoters and literary scholars and historians regarding the perceived value of these films. The latter group, on the whole, distanced themselves from film adaptations of literature and history; revelling in their

---

[46] See 'Phantom Adaptations: *Eucalyptus*, the Adaptation Industry and the Film That Never Was', *Adaptation* 1 (1), 2008, 5–23, 6.

sense of superiority, engagement with film adaptations of canonical literature or historical figures took the form of sneering at their inaccuracies and omissions, a form of analysis that can still be felt today.

To return to *Singin' in the Rain*, the film's title comes from a 1929 song, performed in *The Hollywood Music Box Revue* and *The Hollywood Revue* of 1929, and it encapsulates the nature of the talkie's presence between 1927 and 1937: the defiantly irreverent, frivolous and uplifting *singin'*, voice set against the incongruous backdrop of the Depression. It is all too easy to forget that these films were made during a period of economic, social and political turmoil, at the end of the Prohibition (lifted in 1933), during The Great Depression (resulting from the 1929 stock market crash), the election of Franklin Delano Roosevelt in 1933 and the introduction of New Deal domestic programmes, and at a time which saw the appointment of Hitler as Chancellor of Germany (1933), the imposition of the anti-Jewish Nuremberg Laws (1935) and the beginning of the Spanish Civil War (1936). Hollywood was not impervious to the Depression and the exploitation of workers created tensions between producers and unions, which reached its peak in the post-war period. Many actors in the first decade of sound, including Fredric March, Katherine Hepburn and Jean Muir, were reported to have 'dangerous' left-wing leanings and it would be naïve to consider that all the cast and crew in every production were singing from the same hymn sheet in unison with the conservative ethos of the film studios.

This period saw what James Naremore has described as 'a great appetite for literature among Hollywood moguls, who provided a source of major income, if not artistic satisfaction, for every important playwright and author in the United States'.[47] But while literary writing in this period, such as that of Aldous Huxley and William Faulkner, rooted in the present, warn against the threat of modernity in the new technologies, Hollywood film adaptations of literary works, on the whole, look to the past for their narratives while embracing the technological innovations of the present. In this period, film adaptations, through the help of their promotional materials, earn a reputation for being safe, regressive and sycophantic, an inferior form of cinema that can

[47] Naremore 'Introduction', 4.

never hope to compete with its literary or theatrical precursors or the more innovative cinema of the contemporary period.

Finally, for the sake of manageability, this book will concentrate on American English-speaking adaptations. It is a lamentable fact that Hollywood films of this period seem largely oblivious to the plight of Afro-Americans who are only allowed to appear at the margins of the movies. And the book also recognizes throughout that sound brought with it a loss to cinema's global language. Even though many films were made in more than one language (*Dracula*, for example, was filmed in both English and Spanish) and in other national cinemas, the English-speaking American talkie dominated. Writer and film critic Cedric Belfrage recalls a great loss for him 'was that the international language was over. This was really a thing which nobody seemed to notice very much, but after all, the human species had lived on the face of the globe for a number of years and they had never had a language in which they could all speak to each other, which could be shown everywhere, and which everyone could understand. We just blew it up. And it was really rather sad'.[48] Lamentably, the majority of adaptations produced by the Hollywood major studios are about white middle-class characters who speak exclusively in English and with American or British accents.

On the surface, the new technology of sound produces adaptations that all too easily can be dismissed as overly reliant on theatre and conservative in style and content. Accordingly, these popular talkie adaptations are derided by serious film and literary critics as narrowly focused, backward looking and formulaic, although some of these films, because of the very fact that adaptations of classic stories and historical figures are regarded as such, can afford to be just the opposite.

---

[48] Quoted in Scott Eyman, *The Speed of Sound: Hollywood and the Talkie Revolution, 1926–1930* (Baltimore and London: Johns Hopkins University Press, 1997), 378–9.

2

Sound Shakespeare

Perhaps the most demanding challenge for film adaptation in the first decade of sound was Shakespeare. Sound afforded film a chance to adapt not just Shakespeare's stories, but to reproduce his words for the first time; and the manner in which the words were reproduced was met, on the whole, with disapproval, from both critics of Shakespeare and the movie-going public, what F.R. Leavis would define as minority culture and mass civilization. Shakespeare films, of this period, were regarded as neither cultural products nor entertainment, but somewhere in the gap between the two, a place inhabited by the vast majority of adaptations of canonical literature (neither belonging to English or Film Studies) for most of the twentieth century.

This chapter considers the marketing and reception of Shakespeare adaptations from 1929 to 1937: Sam Taylor's *Taming of the Shrew* (1929 – both directed and written by Taylor), Max Reinhardt and William Dieterle's *A Midsummer Night's Dream* (1935 – adapted by Charles Kenyon and Mary C McCall Jr), George Cukor's *Romeo and Juliet* (1936 – adapted by Talbot Jennings) and Paul Czinner's *As You Like It* (1936 – with a treatment by J.M. Barrie, a scenario by R.J. Cullen and an uncredited adaptation by Carl Mayer), films covertly recalled in the retro silent film, *The Artist* (Michel Hazanavicius, 2011), in which a voice-test of a leading actress, reading from Shakespeare, is dismissed by the uncontrollable laughter of the stubbornly silent leading man. The coming of sound to Shakespeare movies is accurately represented here; it was met with a mixture of anxiety, amusement and contempt, possibly the reason why Louis B. Mayer, head of Metro-Goldwyn-Mayer Studios,

This chapter is an expansion of two short essays which provided the impetus for this book, appearing in *A Companion to Literature, Film and Adaptation*, ed. Deborah Cartmell (Oxford: Blackwell, 2012), 70–84, and *Screening Text: Critical Perspectives on Film Adaptation*, ed. Shannon Wells-Lassagne and Ariane Hudelet (Jefferson and London: McFarland, 2013), 9–21.

reportedly proclaimed that Shakespeare films were 'box office poison'.[1] The stakes were loaded against early talking Shakespeare films: unlike their silent predecessors, talking Shakespeare films ostracized a global audience through the employment of complicated English, insulted 'purists' who insisted that Shakespeare be spoken in full and with an English accent and outraged cineastes who regarded Shakespeare's language and theatrical expression as damaging to the development of cinema. Sound was bad news for the Shakespeare film and by association, film adaptation. No matter how they were pronounced, changed or ignored, words – or more precisely, long, archaic, obscure, unpronounceable or thought-provoking words – were a guarantee of box office failure, at least in the first decade of the sound film.

The Taming of the Shrew, 1929: 'the first ever' adaptation of Shakespeare

There is surprisingly hardly any critical attention given to the coming of sound in the first ever talkie Shakespeare: Sam Taylor's *Taming of the Shrew* (1929). While clearly chosen as a star vehicle for the most famous couple of the silent period, Mary Pickford and Douglas Fairbanks, as a play ultimately concerned with the silencing of a woman, it can be regarded as both a peculiar and appropriate choice for the first mainstream film to give Shakespeare back (some of) his words. The fetishization of this adaptation through its employment of Shakespeare's language becomes the unique selling point of the film in its publicity materials, a feature that bestows upon this adaptation, and its successors, perhaps for the first time, its very credentials as an adaptation. The film marks an important point in the history of screen adaptation and in Shakespeare and screen studies.

    One of sound film's more famous opponents was Aldous Huxley who outspokenly attacked the talkies in his journalism as well as in his novel *Brave New World* (1932). While inviting comparisons with Shakespeare's *Tempest* in its title, implicitly identifying itself as an adaptation of Shakespeare, Huxley's

---

[1]   Quoted in Robert F. Willson, Jr, *Shakespeare in Hollywood 1929–1956* (Madison, WI: Fairleigh Dickinson University Press, 2000), 7.

novel savages film adaptation of Shakespeare through 'the feelies' (or the recently introduced 'talkies'); *Othello* becomes debased and unrecognizable as '*Three Weeks in a Helicopter*, "AN ALL-SUPER-SINGING, SYNTHETIC-TALKING, COLOURED, STEREOSCOPIC FEELY. WITH SYNCHRONIZED SCENT-ORGAN ACCOMPANIMENT".[2] Following from what many of Huxley's contemporaries regarded as the debasing vulgarity of the 'talkies' were the 'smellies', enthusiastically anticipated by an author or authors writing under the pseudonym 'John Scotland' in a monograph, published in 1930, welcoming and explaining the technology of the talkies: 'In America the "Smellies" have actually arrived, and the firm of Metro Goldwin Meyer are claiming to be the pioneers of the latest pandering to yet a further sense.' According to Scotland, the idea of ' "atmospheric" cinema theatres is taking hold and just around the corner'.[3] The 'smellies' were a long way off – and mercifully forgotten today – but the 'talkies' were beginning to take hold and given that Taylor's film was the only mainstream Shakespeare talkie released at the time in which Huxley is writing, it is possible that it is *The Shrew* that is being satirized here as part of the 'brave new world.' The repulsively seductive and debasing experience produced by this adaptation echoes Aldous Huxley's feeling of nausea after watching *The Jazz Singer* – 'I felt ashamed of myself for listening to such things, for even being a member of the species to which such things are addressed.'[4] In spite of his initial repugnance to the talkies, within a few years Huxley, like most of his literary contemporaries, warmed to the art of screenwriting, even settling down in Hollywood as an adaptor himself.

Not all literary critics saw cinema, in particular, the talkie, as threatening, parasitic and patronizing. As I have noted, in 1936, Renaissance scholar Allardyce Nicoll optimistically saw film not just as the new Literature but as 'the new Shakespeare', and in sound, new possibilities for cinema. Paraphrasing Will Hays, Nicoll claims that the recognition of film 'by the great universities' will mark 'the beginning of a new day in motion picture work, paving the way for the motion picture's Shakespeares'.[5] For Nicoll, cinema, especially,

2   Aldous Huxley, *Brave New World* (London: Vintage Press, 2004), 145.
3   John Scotland, *The Talkies* (London: Crosby Lockwood and Son, 1930), 149.
4   Aldous Huxley, 'Silence Is Golden', in *Authors on Film*, ed. Harry M. Geduld (Bloomington, IN: Indiana University Press, 1972), 68–76, 73.
5   Allardyce Nicoll, *Film and Theatre* (London: George G. Harrap, 1936), 163.

the talkie, potentially offers a window into the past, in the uncertain age of modernity, a vehicle for a return to an 'authentic' version of Shakespeare. At the time, Nicoll, as an academic, was in a minority in his enthusiasm for introducing film studies into academia and in his defence of the talking picture, indeed of the Shakespeare adaptation. The bringing of words to Shakespeare films occurred within a climate in which both adaptations and talkies were met with scorn from literary and film critics alike. An adaptation, as Nicoll observes, is doomed as impure cinema:[6] too popular, too commercial and too dependent upon literature and theatrical traditions to be of any value as 'art'. Huxley was not the only one to identify Shakespeare 'talkies' as implicitly the most despicable form of film. As Neil Forsyth has argued, so too did art historian Erwin Panofsky in the much discussed essay, 'Style and Medium in the Moving Pictures' (revised version published in 1947). Panofsky, like Nicoll, singled out the Reinhardt–Dieterle film of *A Midsummer Night's Dream* (1935), which he condemns at great length as 'the most unfortunate film ever produced'[7] in its falling victim to the pitfalls of the 'talkies', in its over-reliance on theatrical rather than filmic traditions.[8] Rather than provide film with artistic kudos, the use of Shakespeare's language (and by implication, that of other canonical writers) is seen not to uplift (as has often been argued), but to devalue cinema. Curiously, there is little, if no mention of an earlier Shakespeare film in academic debates on the talkie adaptation. Given that Sam Taylor's *The Taming of the Shrew* (1929) is the first feature-length Shakespeare 'talkie', it deserves a very special place within the canon of Shakespeare on screen and within the history of film adaptation.[9]

Overshadowed by the Reinhardt–Dieterle film of 1935, surprisingly Taylor's *Shrew* has not been read in relation to its use of sound in the little scholarship devoted to it, a peculiarity given the context in which it was

---

6   Nicoll, 124.

7   Erwin Panofsky, 'Style and Medium in the Moving Pictures', in *Film Theory and Film Criticism: Introductory Essays*, 4th ed., eds. Gerald Mast, Marshall Cohen and Leo Braudy (Oxford: Oxford University Press, 1974), 233–48, 238 .

8   Neil Forsyth 'Shakespeare and the Talkies', in *The Seeming and the Seen: Essays in Modern Visual and Literary Culture*, eds. Beverly Maeder, Jürg Schwyter, Ilona Sigrist and Boris Vejdovsky (Bern: Peter Lang, 2006), 79–102.

9   As Kenneth Rothwell points out, the first 'talkie' of a Shakespeare play was a ten-minute trial scene from *The Merchant of Venice* in 1927. *A History of Shakespeare on Screen: A Century of Film and Television* (Cambridge: Cambridge University Press, 1999), 29.

produced. The film's notoriety is down to its infamous credit line, 'by William Shakespeare with additional dialogue by Samuel Taylor,' and, possibly, for this reason, largely overlooked in Shakespeare and film scholarship. Roger Manvell, in *Shakespeare & the Film* (1971), devotes only two and a half pages to it, citing anecdotal evidence of the film's designer, Laurence Irving's (son of the famous Henry Irving) attempts to persuade Taylor not to make himself a laughing stock by adopting the credit.[10] While the film is still best known for its credit line, there is no evidence that it was ever used and close scrutiny of the film reveals only a few 'additional' lines.[11] Samuel Crowl gives it short shrift in his survey of Shakespeare films, preferring like those before him to concentrate on the 1935 *Midsummer Night's Dream*.[12] The scant attention the film has received, rather than contextualizing it within the new sound era, instead focuses on gender. Russell Jackson has argued that Mary Pickford's wink to Bianca at the end of her lecture on wifely obedience brings Katherine into the twentieth century, making Petruchio the one who is duped.[13] Barbara Hodgdon, on the other hand, sees Katherine's momentary triumph allayed by the alleged cruel treatment of her by her co-star (her husband, Douglas Fairbanks) while on set and in the final moments when Petruchio 'stops her mouth' (to paraphrase from *Much Ado*) with a final forced kiss.[14] Diana E. Henderson is somewhere in the middle in her reading: Katherine becomes 'the sneaky servant rather than the Stepford wife of patriarchy'.[15] Taylor uses leading actors Mary Pickford and Douglas Fairbanks together in the title

[10] Roger Manvell, *Shakespeare & Film* (London: J.M. Dent, 1971), 24–5.

[11] Thomas A. Pendleton notes that the print of the film in the Museum of Modern Art (Fairbanks' copy) contains no tagline and very little additional dialogue. According to Pendleton, additions include 'O Petruchio, beloved' (after Katherine hurls a stool at Petruchio's head), her howl passing for 'I do' at the wedding and lines lifted from Garrick's adaptation of the play. At the end of the wooing scene and after arriving at Petruchio's estate, Katherine states: 'Look to your seat, Petruchio, or I throw you / Cath'rine shall tame this haggard; or if she fails / shall tie her tongue up and pare down her nails.' Thomas Pendleton, '*The Taming of the Shrew*, by Shakespeare and Others,' *PMLA* 108 (1993): 152–3.

[12] Samuel Crowl, *Shakespeare and Film: A Norton Critical Guide* (New York: Norton, 2008).

[13] Russell Jackson, 'Shakespeare's Comedies on Film', in *Shakespeare and the Moving Image*, eds. Anthony Davies and Stanley Wells (Cambridge: Cambridge University Press, 1994), 99–120, 112 . See also *Shakespeare & the English-speaking Cinema* (Oxford: Oxford University Press, 2014), 70.

[14] Barbara Hodgdon, *The Shakespeare Trade: Performances & Appropriations* (Philadelphia, PA: University of Pennsylvania Press, 1998), 15.

[15] Diana E. Henderson, 'A Shrew for the Times, Revisited', in *Shakespeare the Movie II: Popularizing the Plays on Film, TV, Video and DVD*, eds. Richard Burt and Lydna E. Boose (New York: Routledge, 2004), 120–39, 125.

roles for the first time. Undeniably a star vehicle, the film can be seen to expose voyeuristically and exploit their well-known relationship (which, unknown to the audience, was troubled at the time of shooting). The actors' success in the silent period (Pickford was exceedingly well known as 'America's sweetheart,' while Fairbanks' fame was based on his death-defying athleticism and masculinity) is referenced throughout the film. Fairbanks runs everywhere at amazing pace, demonstrates superhuman strength and agility in restraining Katherine and picks up and hurls his servants around as if they're made of feathers. Pickford is continually shown in quintessentially Pickfordesque poses, especially in close-up, emphasizing her famous bow-shaped lips and with quivering eyes looking pleadingly at the camera.

Released simultaneously as a talkie and a silent film,[16] this is a very pared-down version of Shakespeare's play. In the film, the central pair find that their love of brandishing whips is something that they have in common; on meeting Petruchio for the first time, Katherine gazes at Petruchio's exceptionally long and heavy whip and instantaneously hides her much smaller weapon behind her back;[17] or as the pressbook stresses: 'Her whip, which had lashed the back of many a suitor, looked small and puny when compared to his blacksnake.'[18] The whips function as visual correlatives to the whip-like tongues of the central pair, with undeniably phallic associations.

As Ann Thompson has observed in the 1984 Cambridge edition of *The Taming of the Shrew*, David Garrick's 1754 adaptation, which prevailed until the mid-nineteenth century (and upon which this film is based), included a line indicating that Petruchio 'shook his Whip in Token of his Love' and a whip was later added as a property by John Kemble in his 1788 production.[19] According to Thompson, the whip became a standard property for future stage performances, but the Taylor film extends the significance of the whips by including the property in virtually every frame of the movie. Katherine

---

[16] Willson Jr, 19–20.

[17] Maria Jones has pointed out some confusion over the whips in the film. Jackson argues that Katherine throws Petruchio's whip into the fire, thereby disarming him while Hodgdon sees Katherine as throwing her own whip into the fire in an act of capitulation. 'His' or 'Hers?' The Whips in Sam Taylor's *The Taming of the Shrew*', *Shakespeare Bulletin*, 18, 2000, 36–7.

[18] *Taming of the Shrew*, Pressbook (1929), 10.

[19] Ann Thompson, 'Introduction', in *The Taming of the Shrew*, ed. Ann Thompson (Cambridge: Cambridge University Press, 1984), 19.

carries hers around as if it is a handbag. Easily recalled as 'the film with the whips,' these seemingly gratuitous strips of leather are the dominant image of the film, and while the whips can be explained as signifiers of the central characters' sadomasochistic sexuality, their use can be interpreted as a means of achieving discipline and silence: a whip, of course, is a word used to refer to both a person who ensures discipline and a call issued to stamp out deviance in the interests of harmony. It seems a peculiar accident, if it is an accident, that the first mainstream Shakespeare 'talkie' is an adaptation of a play concerned not with the celebration of words but with the suppression of words, and that it makes this theme blatantly apparent through the extensive use of the silence-inducing whips.

But the film's pressbook repeatedly emphasizes that this is a talkie. While contemporary 'so-called serious' writers on film condemn sound movies as popular, formulaic and infantilizing, unsurprisingly the writers of the pressbook, whose motives are purely to sell the movie, continually stress the uplifting quality of sound. Numerous articles in the very detailed pressbook for the film, while overly keen to praise, inadvertently allude to anxieties about the film's reception in its capacity as an 'all-talking' adaptation of Shakespeare. Indeed, the publicity materials covertly address the anticipated criticisms of the likes of Aldous Huxley and Erwin Panofsky. The book arms itself against purist objections to the production of a talking Shakespeare film by directly and audaciously addressing the question of fidelity. In brief, the message of the pressbook is that sound allows for the first time fidelity on screen.

The most striking notion to emerge from the pressbook is its perception of *The Taming of the Shrew* not just as the first mainstream talking adaptation of Shakespeare but as *the first* adaptation of Shakespeare (obliterating all silent predecessors). The pressbook reiterates in its summaries that this is the first film adaptation of the play: 'in this screen story of the Bard's immortal comedy, brought to the screen for *the first* time in the history of motion pictures'[20] or 'the glorious comedy which has come finally to motion pictures after four centuries of success on the legitimate stage.'[21]

[20] Pressbook, 9 (my italics).
[21] Ibid., 10.

It could be argued that the publicity writers failed to do their research or refused to acknowledge earlier adaptations of the play (1908, 1911, 1923, the first directed by D. W. Griffith). But it is more likely that these adaptations were not forgotten but cunningly disqualified as adaptations due to their lack of words. Mary Pickford herself echoes the repeated assertion – 'Shakespeare brought to the screen for the first time'[22] – in an interview by Julian Arthur:

> Also there is another reason why we wanted to be the first to bring Shakespeare to the screen. It somehow seems an advance towards a higher standard in talkie dialogue, and there is something really worthwhile and constructive in this idea. The great mass of people who are unfamiliar with Shakespeare will be introduced to him in a manner that will make his work attractive. We have spared no pains to preserve authenticity in every detail and we have lost none of the spirit of the play in the transcription.[23]

Pickford (or someone pretending to be Pickford) claims that Taylor, Fairbanks and herself are 'the first to bring Shakespeare to the screen,' declaring again that what went before was definitely not Shakespeare. The pressbook repeatedly asserts that this is an adaptation for the very reason that it contains the words of the adapted text.

Pickford's reported speech contains a number of well-known arguments for the justification of filming Shakespeare: to uplift the value of film; to bring culture to the masses; and to somehow capture 'the spirit' of the original. Clearly, the film's producers anticipated that the latter point would be contentious and the pressbook has a number of articles reassuring us of the film's authenticity. In short, it is the words that constitute the film's 'authenticity.' Beginning with the catchline, 'The big three – Mary, Doug, and Bill',[24] the pressbook features an imaginary interview with 'the big three' with Pickford, Fairbanks and Shakespeare pictured drinking tea, discussing the movie.

Fairbanks opens with the introduction, 'Mary, this is Bill Shakespeare. He wrote our last picture'[25] and goes on, with the help of Mary, to convince Shakespeare that if he were alive in 1929, he would be writing for the

---

22 Ibid.
23 Ibid., 15.
24 Ibid., 4.
25 Ibid., 5.

movies and that this film of his play is 'better the way we have shortened it'.[26] The imaginary interview alleviates any fears that the film is a departure from the 'real Shakespeare', with Shakespeare himself giving it the thumbs up and Fairbanks concluding: 'a lot of people have said they wondered what Shakespeare would say about our doing him on the screen. I am certainly glad he dropped in and now I can tell everybody that he is perfectly satisfied'.[27] In another article in the pressbook, 'Adapting Shakespeare to the Talking Picture Screen,' Arthur J. Zellner declares that 'orthodox worshippers of Shakespeare who clothe his every word with an aura of sanctity should not take offense',[28] pointing out some examples of successful theatrical truncated versions, such as Garrick's (whose eighteenth-century production, *Catherine and Petruchio*, is claimed as inspiration for the film). Critic James Agate writing in *The London Pavilion* (1929) introduces the film to cinema audiences, confidently averring that 'it is safe to say that if the cinema had been known in Shakespeare's day, there is nothing in the present picture which Shakespeare would have disowned.'[29]

The pressbook mixes pseudo scholarship with tabloid-style journalism, clearly in anticipation of attacks from Shakespearean 'purists', the likes of Aldous Huxley, who will not abide Shakespeare's words being spoken on film. As mentioned earlier, the dominant theme of the pressbook is the film's fidelity to Shakespeare, a subject quite clearly instigated by the use of sound in this production. Repeatedly, we are told that *all* the words are those of Shakespeare:

> ...not one bit of the glorious Shakespearean dialogue has been sacrificed when in keeping with the fast moving comedy, director Sam Taylor has re-told the story with the deftness so characteristic of his work....[30]

> Every line of dialogue used in the picture stands as written by the Bard himself.[31]

---

[26] Ibid.
[27] Ibid.
[28] Ibid., 30. He loses some credibility when he refers to 'the stilted phrases of the 15th century' (16).
[29] James Agate, *London Pavilion*, no. 768, November 11, 1929.
[30] Pressbook, 10.
[31] Ibid.

…every bit of dialogue spoken in the film was taken from the original Shakespeare and every bit of atmosphere, from the characters to the sets, is in keeping with the customs of the fifteenth century.[32]

These repeated assertions of pure authenticity seem to have been swallowed by contemporary reviewers, in spite of the publicists' ignorance (in the passage quoted above) of the very period in which Shakespeare was writing.

Figure 2.1 Pressbook, *Taming of the Shrew*, 1929

Without doubt, the sound by today's standards is dreadful, with Pickford and Fairbanks shouting out all their lines with little trace of emotion. Pickford claimed to be disappointed with her own performance, retiring from acting shortly after making the film; rather than presenting Katherine as an equal to Petruchio in strength and wit, she felt that she played the part like a 'spitting kitten'.[33] Most critics have claimed that Fairbanks steals the show,

[32] Ibid.
[33] Willson, 26.

with Pickford looking uncomfortable and out of place throughout.[34] But this discomfort is with the spoken words and strikingly, all the emotion in the film is conveyed in the nonspeaking sections, as Taylor's film oscillates between the talkie and silent modes, very much a film aware of its transitional and dual status. Given the talkie was seen as a purely commercial enterprise and despised by those advocates of pure cinema and literary critics who saw the coming of sound as a further invasion and violation of their artistic territory, the contrasting styles, the talkie and the silent, are indeed pertinent. It is worth noting that the sound version of the film is framed by much talking while the middle section is dominated by silence that 'upstages' the overly theatrical opening and closing. The shouting of the central actors is in sharp contrast to the superiority of their silent performances.

Significantly, the first mainstream Shakespeare talkie is a play about the 'successful' suppression of the dangerous female tongue, as mentioned, blatantly visualized by the whips in this production. But it is a success that is not altogether unqualified, given that Katherine finds a voice (albeit one that is music to the ears of a patriarchal society) at the end of the play. The film on one level exploits the fame of the central couple while on another self-consciously juxtaposes the visual with the verbal, the silent film with the talkie. Surprisingly, in the sound/image war, silence wins over words in the final impression of the film as Katherine's spectating is far more eloquent than Petruchio's verbal declarations. Take the scene in which Petruchio sends Katherine to bed and returns to eat the rejected food. Diana E. Henderson's observation that Katherine 'remains the one who sees more than her husband, creating a silent connection between her perspective and the filmmaker's own'[35] can be extended into regarding the film's oppositional aesthetics: Katherine sees and Petruchio talks, reflecting the debate, here a veritable battle, between silent and talking cinema.

Katherine, after miraculously undergoing a makeover from a mud-soaked and bedraggled wreck to a perfectly groomed starlet complete with diaphanous white peignoir, opens the bedroom door and gazes down

---

[34] See Hodgdon.
[35] Henderson, 125.

at Petruchio who is at the table with his dog, Troilus. At this point of the film, Katherine has been transformed from bad to good girl, symbolized in the change of costume from black riding suit (worn at the outset of the film) to pure white. Positioned at the top of the staircase, she literally and metaphorically looks down at Petruchio. Unable to speak, she is visually superior and given a voice in her enforced silence, and in contrast to Shakespeare's Katherine her tactical advantage enables her to triumph over this Petruchio's unguarded scheming:

> PETRUCHIO:
> *Troilus, good dog for a hearty meal*
> Thus have I politicly begun my reign,
> And *it is* my hope to end successfully.
> *Today* she ate no meat *and today she shall not sleep.*
> Last night she slept not, nor tonight she shall not.
> As with the meat, some fault
> I'll find about the making of the bed,
> And here I'll fling the pillow, there the bolster,
> This way the coverlet, another way the sheets.
> And *amidst* this hurly I *pretend*
> That all is done in *loving* care of her;
> And *then forsooth she'll* watch all night,
> And if she chance to nod I'll rail and *sing*,
> And with *my singing* keep her still awake.
> This is *the* way to kill a wife with kindness,
> And thus I'll curb her mad and headstrong humour.
> *Does thou know* better how to tame a shrew.
> [Dog barks]
>   *Nay, good Troilus, nay. (The Taming of the Shrew*, 1939)[36]

The eavesdropping Katherine speaks visually throughout the sequence, gradually moving from the shock of the spectacle to plotting revenge (in anticipation of the finale, concluding with a knowing wink to the camera).

---

[36] The italics indicate where words have been changed or added. For instance 'pretend' replaces 'intend', 'loving' replaces 'reverend' and 'sing' replaces 'brawl'. The text is taken from the soundtrack and compared to *The Taming of the Shrew*, 4.1, 177–99. This speech is not in Garrick's *Catherine and Petruchio*. From *The Taming of the Shrew*, ed. Barbara Hodgdon (Methuen: London, 2010).

Petruchio, oblivious to the fact he is being watched and overheard, brags to the dog (which has physically and symbolically taken Katherine's place at the table). The juxtaposition of the two characters, one silent and the other carelessly and unnecessarily wordy, reflects the film's transitional status between silent cinema and talkie. Clearly, the more eloquent of the two is Katherine and in the debate between what Gilbert Seldes refers to as 'the talkies' and 'the movies', the talkie is shown to be vastly inferior: stupid, infantile and lacking in subtlety due to its unnecessary wordiness.[37] Against the grain of the pressbook's valorization of the wordiness of Taylor's *The Taming of the Shrew*, the film seems to be at pains to reinforce the old adage that a picture speaks louder than words or that the central pair, especially Pickford, are making a final and fruitless plea for the survival of silent cinema in anticipation that the new talkie will end both careers. Retrospectively, Pickford lamented in her autobiography: 'The making of that film was my finish. My confidence was completely shattered, and I was never again at ease before the camera or microphone.'[38]

This is Shakespeare with and without words: Katherine is 'silenced' (as Pickford writes in her autobiography she was asked to adopt Pickfordian characteristics in her portrayal of Kate)[39] and while Petruchio's words are victorious, sound is vastly outplayed by silence and the end product is in direct opposition to the publicity surrounding it. (Significantly, Sam Taylor himself makes no contribution to the pressbook and its valorization of words.) Claims that this is the first ever Shakespeare film and declarations about its fidelity to Shakespeare in its preservation of the words are contradicted by the primacy of the visual over the verbal, or the silent film over the talking adaptation. Indeed the film itself, contrary to the message of the pressbook, seems to fight against its status as an adaptation, or that of an 'all-talking' film.

---

[37] Cultural commentator Gilbert Seldes distinguished between 'movies' and 'talkies', the latter often 'a chaos distasteful to the orderly mind', *An Hour with the Movies and the Talkies* (London: J.P. Lippincott Co.), 1929, 8.

[38] Quoted in Henderson, 124.

[39] As Jackson (20) and Henderson (124) note, Pickford claims in her autobiography, *Sunshine and Shadow* (1956), she was told to rely on her silent tricks rather than attempt something more dramatic.

The Taming of the Shrew's pressbook audaciously reveals that the coming of sound enabled the birth of adaptation and while the promoters of the film do their utmost to proclaim the film as an adaptation, indeed the first Shakespeare adaptation ever, the film itself does the opposite, demonstrating the superior eloquence of silence. While the pressbook of *The Taming of the Shrew* repeatedly marvels at Shakespeare's words on screen, the image of the whips suggests throughout that this is a film that fiercely asks its characters to 'shut up.'

Shakespeare shorts and *A Midsummer Night's Dream*, 1935

The acquisition of sound, or more precisely, words, transformed the way that Shakespeare adaptations were regarded in the early sound period and beyond. As I have argued, Sam Taylor's *Taming of the Shrew* (the first mainstream Shakespeare talkie of 1929) enacts a flirtatious tussle between sound and silent film, especially through its employment of the omnipresent silent-inducing whips that simultaneously make an impressive noise for those seeking the thrills of sound cinema while asking the Shakespearean speakers to be silent. The Shakespeare films that followed in the thirties (while seemingly wilfully forgetting the existence of the earlier *Taming of the Shrew*) made similar claims about their position as the first adaptations of the plays (and the necessity of speaking the author's words to qualify as an adaptation) while simultaneously reflecting anxieties about the introduction of Shakespeare's words into mass media entertainment.

The extraordinarily daring *Taming of the Shrew* (in its covert plea for a return to silence) did much to warn off any further attempts to film Shakespeare during the following years. As Scott Eyman has observed, the film was the beginning of the end for its stars Mary Pickford and Douglas Fairbanks,[40] a film which provided a cautionary tale for all stars of the silent screen not to aim too high – not to attempt Shakespeare before they had proven that they could talk at all. Indeed, shortly after its release the film was

---

[40] *The Speed of Sound* (Baltimore, MD: Johns Hopkins University Press, 1997), 276.

undeservedly reduced to a laughing stock; according to Scott MacQueen, in the early thirties Hollywood fell to sniggering about the first Shakespearean 'train wreck' of talking cinema.[41] Theodore Dreiser, writing three years after the film's release remembers that 'Douglas Fairbanks was Douglas Fairbanks and none other most of the time; he forgot that Shakespeare wrote this play around a character, Petruchio, and not around himself as an athletic and grimacing motion-picture star.'[42] This attitude to the film, as more Hollywood than Shakespeare, is still prevalent in the relative neglect the film receives in Shakespeare and film criticism, regardless of its status as the first mainstream 'talkie' adaptation of Shakespeare, not to mention the audacious claim in the publicity materials that this is the first ever Shakespeare film adaptation.

It was not until 1935 that another major Shakespeare adaptation appeared: Max Reinhardt and William Dieterle's *A Midsummer Night's Dream*, produced by Warner Brothers, featuring the contract actors of the company, including James Cagney (Bottom), Olivia de Havilland (Hermia), Dick Powell (Lysander), Joe E. Brown (Flute) and Mickey Rooney (Puck). But prior to the extravaganza of *Dream* there were some shorter and less adventurous attempts at talking Shakespeare. 1929 saw each studio presenting a variety act film, each showcasing its big stars and newly found talking abilities. Two of these attempted Shakespeare. Norma Shearer appears as Juliet in MGM's *Hollywood Revue* (1929) followed by John Barrymore as Richard III in Warner Brothers' *Show of Shows* (1929), both performances are amidst an array of vaudeville, acrobatic, music and comedy acts. Both performances situate Shakespeare in relation to popular entertainment, a sign of things to come. *The Show of Shows* presents a talking John Barrymore as Richard III on top of a hill of bodies (one disturbingly moves at the end of the sequence); his dramatic, highly theatrical recitation is preceded (and undermined) by an introduction in which we're informed that Richard will dispose of his enemies 'with the graceful impartiality of Al Capone.'[43]

---

[41] Scott MacQueen, audio commentary on *A Midsummer Night's Dream*, 1935, DVD, Turner Entertainment Co and Warner Bros. Entertainment Inc., USA, 2007.

[42] Theodore Dreiser, 'The Hollywood Experience', from *Liberty*, June 11, 1932, reprinted in *Authors on Film*, ed. Harry M. Geduld (Bloomington, IN: Indiana University Press, 1922), 206–22, 213.

[43] *The Show of Shows*, John G. Adolfi, dir., Frank Fay, J. Keirn Brennan, scr., Warner Bros. Pictures, 1929.

Hollywood's efforts to make Shakespeare accessible in the sound era are explicitly mocked in the first of these variety extravaganzas, MGM's *Hollywood Revue*, which features two versions of the balcony scene with Shearer as Juliet and John Gilbert (star of the silent screen and whose career was allegedly ruined by the talkies) as Romeo.[44] After a 'straight' rendition of the scene, the pair are congratulated by director Lionel Barrymore who simultaneously receives 'a wire from New York' which reads 'don't change a thing, but the main title and the dialogue'; in a film now re-titled, 'The Necker', the two dutifully repeat the scene in 1929 slang ('Now listen, boyfriend you have a nice line in chatter but how do I know you care for me in a big way?'/ 'Julie baby, I'm ga-ga about you'). Dismissed as a 'shrivelling failure' by Scott Eyman,[45] the skit jokingly forecasts that Shakespeare may confront even more insurmountable obstacles than those of the film actors playing him in making the transition from silence to sound.

A Midsummer Night's Dream can be seen to take heed of this warning and on one level, is defiantly anti-theatrical in its choice of cast (none of whom have significant theatrical pedigrees), deliberately employing a decidedly cinematic style of acting. A similar 'wire' to that sent in the 1929 *Hollywood Revue* was delivered to Irving Asher, head of Warner Brothers' London studio, asking that the play be rendered 'more colloquial' for the 1935 film.[46] Accompanied by Mendelssohn's *Midsummer Night's Dream*, the trailer begins 'America applauded! Europe cheered! Asia thrilled! The whole world hailed this screen masterpiece! And paid $2.20 to see it. Now at last it comes to you at popular prices.' The trailer stresses the film's democratic credentials, appealing to a global audience, oblivious to its use of Shakespeare's notoriously difficult language, and emphasizes its cheapness (compared to premiere prices), so as to capitalize on film's potential to provide culture for next to nothing. (Indeed a major departure from the play, is the democratization of the *dramatis personae*, with Bottom – played by James Cagney – reinvented as a character to be applauded rather than laughed at for his social presumptuousness.) As it

---

44 This sequence is available on YouTube, http://www.youtube.com/watch?v=vbMDp8OkU7E (Accessed 19/02/12).
45 *The Speed of Sound*, 315.
46 Scott MacQueen, audio commentary on *A Midsummer Night's Dream*.

has been argued, the choice of the play, on one level, may be a response to the imposition of censorship on the cinema (with Warner Brother productions very much on the defensive in their alleged glorification of violence through their popular gangster films from which Cagney established his reputation); normally thought of as one of Shakespeare's 'safer' plays, this adaptation brings themes of sexual violence and repression disturbingly to the forefront of the production, commencing with the explicit allusions to Hippolyta's violent abduction by Theseus and ending with a menacing Puck (played by a teenage Mickey Rooney) sneakily following Theseus and Hippolyta into their bedroom at the film's conclusion; these themes of enslavement or imprisonment and perverse surveillance could strike a chord at a time in which Jewish filmmakers, including Rienhardt and Dieterle, were banned from working in Germany.

One aspect of this film forgotten today is the fact that it was made within the first decade of sound cinema and that like its predecessor, *The Taming of the Shrew*, it juxtaposes verbal with non-verbal sequences in a playful confrontation between the two styles. The 1935 film begins with a possible allusion to the 1929 film in the figure of the silenced Hippolyta. Like Katherine at the end of *The Shrew*, Hippolyta is in the last stages of her taming (having been 'wooed by the sword') and she is introduced into the film as what only can be described as a quivering wreck, wearing a tight-fitting chain-mail helmet and a snake entwined around her neck which restrains her right arm in a loose form of a straitjacket. The snake is a possible reference to the whips in *The Taming of the Shrew* and a visual correlative to Oberon's description of Titania's bower where a 'snake throws her enamelled skin, / Weed wide enough to wrap a fairy in' and Hermia's account of her nightmare (revealed to an absent Lysander in which a 'serpent ate my heart away, / And you sat smiling at his cruel prey').[47] While the original screenplay included a prelude or back-story of the conquest of the Amazons by Theseus, the initial impression of Hippolyta here compactly retains the story of a woman who has reluctantly surrendered, now visually crestfallen and conquered.[48] The

---

[47] 2.1. 255–256 and 2.2.155-6, respectively. From *The Complete Works*, ed. Stanley Wells, Gary Taylor, John Jowett and William Montgomery (Oxford: Clarendon Press, 1988).

[48] For an account of this, see Russell Jackson, *Shakespeare Films in the Making: Vision, Production and Reception* (Cambridge: Cambridge University Press, 2007), 28.

back story is also omnipresent throughout the film in Theseus's fantastic palace with its phallic undulating pillars, which Jack J. Jorgens describes as contributing to the film's dark, post-Freudian reading of the play.[49] Allegedy Verree Teasdale, the actress who plays Hippolyta, was heard to exclaim a 'hundred times during the lengthy production', 'my kingdom for the privilege of sitting down for five short minutes'[50] as her first costume contained rings which cut into her flesh if she created too much movement. The life-like snake featured in the first costume reappears as an artificial one in Hippolyta's next appearance, where she wears a dramatic sculpted black and silver dress with an ornamental snake outlining the bodice. While stunningly majestic, she remains a prisoner of the costume. She ends the film in a third dress – a lighter and sparkling gown with pronounced fairy-like ruff. However, Theseus's all too proximate dark-caped figure seems to swallow her up at the pair's departure, possibly recalling the now famous 'Nocturne' sequence in which Oberon's billowing black cape envelopes and brings darkness to the fairy world.

The film's daring, explicitly disturbing opening – like the subject matter of *The Taming of the Shrew* – concerned with the silencing of a woman, is extended throughout this adaptation, in arguably one of the most 'outspoken' of all Shakespeare movies. Without doubt, the most memorable sequence in this film is the 'Nocturne' choreographed by Bronislova Nijinska which thematically mirrors the message of the opening sequence through the invasion of the male fairies and subsequent subduing of Titania. In the play, Oberon – who in the film is depicted in a black jumpsuit full of sparkles, evocative of a 'Prince of Darkness' – opens Titania's eyes to the reality that she is in love with an ass (both Bottom and Oberon himself) and at the same time demanding 'Silence a while' (4.1.79). In the film, he engulfs her with his snake-like black mantle, bringing, with his dark-costumed entourage, a masculine darkness to the world of the female fairies. The stunning sequence is easily the most memorable in the film, a sequence which brings silence to a world of sound, an ominous message for Titania and her troupe; it

---

[49] *Shakespeare on Film* (Bloomington, IN: Indiana University Press, 1977), 51.
[50] 'Shakespearean Art Makes 'Martyrs' of Film Stars', *A Midsummer Night's Dream* Pressbook, 1935, 26.

nonetheless provides a bold and defiant display of how images can speak more eloquently than words, even Shakespeare's words.

The film's use of sound, or of words, was met with a mixed response. Writing for the radical *New Theatre & Film*, 'Charmion Von Wiegand' (names in this left-wing journal were changed in order to protect their authors' positions) lamented how 'Shakespeare is reduced to Ziegfeld Follies in a forest' and complained about filming a Shakespeare play in a time of mass unemployment and with a war looming.[51] Graham Greene praised the cinematic fairy sequence while condemning the spoken poetry as serving merely to delay the action.[52] In other words, Greene liked the action but hated the words. Harley Granville-Barker in 'Alas, Poor Will' (*The Listener*, 1937), ranted that the filmed words 'not merely mutilated, but [were] occasionally even re-written from Elizabethan English into plainer American. What is one to say of such an outrage?'[53] Alfred Hitchcock, while defending the film in opposition to Harley Granville-Barker's 'purist' attack, agreed, too, that the words get in the way and the 'general public will not be talked at'.[54] As mentioned earlier, no one could be more horrified by Shakespeare's words spoken on screen than art historian Erwin Panofsky, who singled out the Reinhardt-Dieterle film of *A Midsummer Night's Dream* (1935) as 'the most unfortunate film ever produced'[55] in its falling victim to the pitfalls of the 'talkies' in its over-reliance on theatrical rather than filmic traditions – that is, its dependence on words.

But the publicity materials proclaim otherwise – the film is regarded as both popular entertainment as well as educationally uplifting. The pressbook insists on the film's pedagogical value, echoing Nicoll's yearning for 'quality' audiences, setting up a club to endorse the film for a certain 'class of people' and it features a section entitled 'Spreading the News Round Schools' with plenty of ideas as to how to inspire youthful attendance at a Shakespeare film without 'forcing it down

---

[51] Charmion Von Wiegand, 'Reinhardt's *Dream*', *New Theatre and Film: 1934–1937* (San Diego, CA and New York: Harcourt Brace, 1985), 279–83, 281.

[52] *The Spectator*, 18 October 1935, in *The Graham Greene Film Reader: Mornings in the Dark*, ed. David Parkinson (Harmondsworth: Penguin, 1993), 38.

[53] *The Listener* XVII, 425, 3 March 1937, 387–9, 387.

[54] 'Much Ado About Nothing', reprinted in *Shakespeare on Film, Television and Radio: The Researcher's Guide*, ed., Olwen Terris, Eve-Marie Oesterlen, Luke McKernan (London: British Universities Film & Video Council, 2009), 145–8.

[55] Panofsky, 233–48, 238.

their throats'.[56] The educational value of the film, marketed at parents, is extended through the production of study guides and teachers' manuals 'for school tie-ups on this picture'[57] and the pressbook even includes a photograph of 'Professor' Reinhardt with the cast, sitting around a table, studying the play. It seems that the pressbook is trying to persuade its readership that this film 'is the real thing' due to the fact that it's speaking Shakespeare's language. Claims of its uniqueness – that this is a first – are not understated in the pressbook. Exhibitors are told 'THREE HOURS OF ENTERTAINMENT THAT WAS THREE CENTURIES IN THE MAKING', 'THE SHOW THAT THE INVENTOR OF MOTION PICTURES DREAMED SOME DAY WOULD BE MADE' and 'WARNER BROS., WHO BROKE THE SILENCE OF THE FILMS WITH TALKING PICTURES, NOW BRINGS THE MIGHTY VOICE OF SHAKESPEARE TO THE SCREEN.'[58] The implied association between Warner Brothers ('WHO BROKE THE SILENCE OF THE FILMS') and Shakespeare's 'MIGHTY VOICE' suggests that this is Shakespeare's language with a modern twist that is accessible to all. Exhibitors are encouraged to lure the public to the movie with statements such as:

> That Shakespeare wrote for all the people rather than any one class is being proven twice a day at _____ Theatre where the Bard's greatest comedy, 'A Midsummer Night's Dream' is playing.
>
> Students of grade schools sit beside professors of literature and taxi drivers touch elbows with dignified solons, in common enjoyment.[59]
>
> Suggestions for reviews include the likes of 'It's the swellest show I ever attended', reported _____ who drives Yellow Taxi No. _____.'[60]

The chief selling point of this film seems to be the accessibility of Shakespeare, with words spoken with a new accent – that is in the language of Hollywood. The trailer celebrates the film's global appeal and cheap prices, the film's stars' introductions to the film proclaim it to be a significant moment in the history of Hollywood; for both Jean Muir (Helena) and Frank McHugh (Quince), the film is 'as new to the talking screen as sound was to the silent'.

---

[56] 'Spreading the News Round Schools, *A Midsummer Night's Dream* Pressbook, 1936, 6.

[57] 'Teachers' Manuals' from Hays Office', Pressbook – see *A Midsummer Night's Dream*, ed. E. Edward Edleson (New York: 1936), 6.

[58] 'Catchlines', Pressbook, 21.

[59] 'All Ages and All Classes Join in Praise of 'Dream', *A Midsummer Night's Dream*, Pressbook, 29.

[60] Pressbook, 29.

Warner Brothers' extraordinarily eccentric and irreverent promotional 20-minute film, *Shake, Mr. Shakespeare*, directed by Roy Mack, goes one stage further, presenting a screenwriter at his desk having been tasked with reading all of Shakespeare following the imagined stupendous overnight success of *A Midsummer Night's Dream*. Faced with the newspaper adverts, 'coming', *Macbeth, Julius Caesar, Othello, Hamlet*, the writer falls asleep and visions appear. Typically 'loud-mouthed' American Shakespearean characters pop out of their books and proceed to 'modernize' their characters so that Romeo sings a ditty ('Romeo and Hollywood, what sublimity / Does anyone know if Miss Garbo / Has a bal-con-y?'), Hamlet performs a jazzy dance sequence backed by a group of Hamletettes and Antony entertains with a song and dance number which begins 'Friends, Romans, and Countrymen, lend me your feet / To the tune we love, the rhythm of Forty-Second Street'. Finally, Shakespeare himself appears, complaining 'Is it for this that I spilled so much magic ink?' and Hamlet concludes, 'today the screenplay is the thing'.[61]

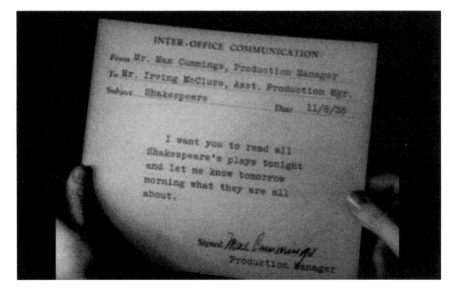

Figure 2.2 Screenshot, *Shake, Mr. Shakespeare* (Warner Brothers, Roy Mack, 1936)

[61] Available on the DVD special features on *A Midsummer Night's Dream*.

Figure 2.3 Screenshot, *Shake, Mr. Shakespeare* (Warner Brothers, Roy Mack, 1936)

The promotional short is *a tour de force* of satire and musical direction, but as an entrée to *A Midsummer Night's Dream*, it could not be further from the film it promotes.

Reinhardt's declared suspicion of American talkies and his prioritizing of the music, as suggested by his desire to keep Erich Wolfgang Korngold – who arranged the music for the film – on the set, intimate that Shakespeare's language was of secondary importance.[62] Indeed the actors were asked to speak to the music, almost as if they were singing their words to Korngold's score. The universal language of music and the emphasis on visuals serve to upstage the words and in this respect, the film harks back to the silent period of film-making in its attempt to appeal to a global audience. The flippancy of the promotional films, especially *Shake, Mr. Shakepeare* insisting on the translation of Shakespeare into 'American', reveals an anxiety about the words and the realization that they would (and did) stand in the way of the film's box office appeal.

[62] Scott MacQueen, audio commentary on *A Midsummer Night's Dream*.

Romeo and Juliet, 1936

Undaunted by the mixed success of *A Midsummer Night's Dream*, the following year saw the release of two other adaptations of Shakespeare: George Cukor's *Romeo and Juliet*, starring Leslie Howard and Norma Shearer, and the British film, *As You Like It*, directed by Paul Czinner, with Laurence Olivier in the role of Orlando. Within the short period of sound cinema, much had changed. While in 1929 promoters of *The Taming of the Shrew* repeatedly boasted verbal authenticity, by 1935 it was clear that words were getting in the way of entertainment. Like the Warners' *Midsummer Night's Dream*, MGM's *Romeo and Juliet* betrays anxieties about promoting the words in its publicity materials, focusing on the universal appeal of the well-known story. Nonetheless, like *A Midsummer Night's Dream* before it, promoters were not shy to boast originality with the pressbook opening with: 'Boy Meets Girl – 1436 – ROMEO AND JULIET – 1936' and followed by the claim that 'now, after five hundred years [*Romeo and Juliet*], has for the first time been transformed in all its beauty and breathless excitement to a medium perfected for its reception – the motion picture screen',[63] thus claiming the film to be the first adaptation of the play in spite of the numerous versions of *Romeo and Juliet* that went before.[64]

The promotional short film *Master Will Shakespeare* (MGM, Jacques Tourneur, 1936) tells the story of Shakespeare's journey to London in search of recognition, made explicitly analogous to those who currently seek their fame and fortune in Hollywood: the voice-over compares Shakespeare's ambitions with Hollywood hopefuls: 'You've heard that call little stage-struck Sally, haven't you? And you too footlight fascinated John, who has a play tucked away as Master Will Shakespeare had'.[65]

While making the obligatory comparisons between Shakespeare's stage and Hollywood film (in particular, the smoking and portly Burbage is unmistakeably

---

[63] Boy Meets Girl - 1436, ROMEO AND JULIET – 1936', *Romeo and Juliet* Pressbook, 1936, np. The authors of this go on to claim that a film of *Romeo and Juliet* was previously impossible, as there was not a producer who could rise to the challenge before Irving Thalberg came along.

[64] The Internet Movie Database lists eleven with matching titles alone.

[65] 'Master Will Shakespeare', Jacques Tourneur, dir., Richard Goldstone, scr., *Romeo and Juliet* (1936), Turner Entertainment Co., 2007.

Figure 2.4 Pressbook, *Romeo and Juliet*, 1936

Figure 2.5 *Master Will Shakespeare* (MGM, Jacques Tourneur, 1936)

evocative of a cigar-smoking Hollywood mogul), the film it promotes, *Romeo and Juliet*, is less 'American' than its predecessor, *A Midsummer Night's Dream*. The mainly British cast (among the most notable exceptions to this is Andy Devine, whose broad American accent was an abomination to British reviewers)[66] was something of a risk. The film's producer, Irving Thalberg (Shearer's husband and model for F. Scott Fitzgerald's Monroe Stahr in *The Last Tycoon*) takes most of the credit for the film which, like *A Midsummer Night's Dream*,[67] is marketed in the trailer through its value for money; first performances were a staggering $2.20 but we are now reassured that the film is available 'at popular prices'. The price distinction between premiere prices and normal seats is shorthand for the marketing of the film as cheap cultural capital, erasing the division between high and low culture, elite and mass entertainment. The cover of the pressbook, as Russell Jackson observes, forecasts the film's (misguided) sense of its marketability: 'The World's Greatest Love Story Becomes Your Guaranteed Box-Office Attraction.'[68] With pictures of the leading pair, Norma Shearer and Leslie Howard, the trailer humorously reduces the plot to a typical Hollywood Romance with 'This Girl, This Boy' (ironically they were aged 33 and 43, respectively).

Their performances are marred – perhaps due to their advanced ages – by an underlying sense of embarrassment throughout and thus the film lacks emotional conviction. The restraint of the central pair may be a response to the Motion Picture Production Code, a reserve reflected in the interior shots, which are cold, clinical and church-like. Juliet's bedroom with pulpit-shaped balcony, her Madonna-like poses and the elaborate Botticelli-inspired but unrevealing costumes contribute to an overall lack of passion. This highly 'respectful treatment' of Shakespeare is evident in the pre-eminence given to the literary consultant, Professor William Strunk, Jr, of Cornell University, in the film's opening credits. For the most part, the language is heavily punctuated with action as if to give viewers a break from the words. Even more pronounced than in *A Midsummer Night's Dream* are the contrasting film styles – wordless, visually stimulating sequences (the dances in Capulet's

[66] Russell Jackson, 159.
[67] Ibid., 46.
[68] Jackson, 154.

feast) with scenes that are heavily theatrical and seem overly wordy (for example John Barrymore's (Mercutio's) Queen Mab speech is spoken with indecent haste, as if to get it over with as quickly as possible). The quietest of all scenes, Juliet's false funeral, is stunningly shot with numerous mourners zigzagging down a dramatic hillside lined with cypress trees.

Harley Granville-Barker regarded the pretension to academic scholarship an offence to Shakespeare. Not deigning to name Professor Strunk, Jr, he refers to 'a gentleman placarded upon the screen as a Literary Advisor'.[69] In writing of this so-called academic, he vents his hostility to the translation of Shakespeare's words to screen: 'Was it he who advised them to leave out more than half the text, or occasionally to hand a speech belonging to one character over to another, or to chop the verse into pieces, and time and time again quite wantonly to cut the rhyme out of the rhymed couplets?'[70] Although poles apart, it is as clear to Granville-Barker as it is to Louis B. Mayer that Shakespeare's words do not mix with film:

> Of the cinema's second-best foot – so to call it – the mechanical reproduction of speech, there is little that need yet be said. The delicate colouring and fine gradations demanded by the speaking of poetry are still beyond its technique (in that filmed 'Romeo and Juliet' a surprising proportion of the inhabitants of Verona seemed indeed to be afflicted with cleft palates). But bring it to perfection, it will still hardly oust the picture side of the cinema from pride of place.[71]

These views, that of the Hollywood mogul and the literary critic, on Shakespeare films as being too wordy and not wordy enough are possibly why Hollywood drew a halt to what Granville-Barker calls 'the mechanical reproduction of [Shakespeare's] speech'. In the mid-thirties there were plans for other Shakespeare films: a Warner Brothers' *Twelfth Night* (directed by Max Reinhardt) and *As You Like It* (from the MGM studios with Shearer suggested as Rosalind and John Barrymore as Jaques) but tellingly there were no further major Shakespeare films until the next decade. As a measure

---

[69] *The Listener*, 388.
[70] Ibid.
[71] Ibid.

of *Romeo and Juliet*'s failure, Leslie Howard's theatre production of *Hamlet* the following year was deemed a flop, eclipsed by the rival John Gielgud performance. Howard failed to cash in on his starring role as Romeo and we can only assume that those who saw him as Romeo did not want a repeat Shakespearean performance.

As You Like It, 1936

Produced in the same year as *Romeo and Juliet*, *As You Like It* rarely gets more than a few words in Shakespeare and film criticism but it deserves to be considered alongside the above films produced between 1929 and 1936 as a Shakespeare product of the new sound era. As with the previous films, there is a noticeable disjunction between the movie itself and how it is marketed; the reverential and serious tone of the production is clearly at odds with the emphasis in the promotional materials on the film's popularity. *As You Like It*, the first major talkie of a Shakespeare play filmed in England (UK: Inter Allied/20th Century Fox), was hailed as a star vehicle for the now virtually forgotten actress Elisabeth Bergner, with co-star Laurence Olivier. This was not the first British Shakespeare talkie film however. A 1935 biopic, *The Immortal Gentleman* (directed by Widgey R. Newman), depicts Shakespeare in a tavern in Southwark, where he observes to Ben Jonson and Michael Drayton, how customers recall characters from his plays. Dismissed as 'as dreadful a film as has ever been made, meanly produced, ill-lit, ill-staged, scarcely directed at all, with some howlingly bad excerpts from the plays … the nadir of filmed Shakespeare', the movie has sunk into oblivion.[72]

As You Like It may have suffered a similar fate, if it were not for the presence of Olivier. Like Norma Shearer, Bergner's role in *As You Like It* may have been compromised by the involvement of her husband (the film's director) and she fails to live up to the hype of the pressbook, which

---

[72] Luke McKernan and Olwen Terris, *Walking Shadows: Shakespeare in the National Film and Television Archive* (London: BFI, 1994), 190 . A brief discussion of this film can be found in Megan Murray-Pepper, 'The "tables of memory": Shakespeare, cinema and the writing desk', *The Writer on Film: Screening Literary Authorship*, ed. Judith Buchanan (Houndmills, Basingstoke: Palagrave, 2013), 92–105, 94–5.

applauds her performance on every page. Although, like its predecessors, the film promoters tried to capitalize on the pedagogical uses of the movie, they were also anxious to attract a global market – the pressbook notes the foreign accent of the star as an asset for universal appeal[73] while the posters and advertisements 'protest too much' about the film's easy intelligibility. A typical 'review', for instance reverts to the film's combination of authenticity and accessibility: 'With an astonishing lack of reverential awe with which everyone ordinarily views Shakespeare, the producers of "As You Like It" have brought the play to the screen as Shakespeare intended it should have been produced in one of the screen's great achievements.'[74] In contrast to the pedagogical activities suggested to exhibitors, the promotional advice featured in the pressbook insistently proclaims 'Highbrow? Art-y? Forget it! Shakespeare is fun'.[75] Cartoon images include two young women in twin beds assessing the film ('BUT DID YOU EVER SEE A MAN LIKE THAT ORLANDO BEFORE? HO-HUM! PLEASANT DREAMS!'), a young boy eagerly accompanying his mother to the film and men at work, with an overly muscular tattooed and toothless builder affirming that *As You Like It* is a film totally suited to his tastes ('YEAH I THINK IT'S FULL OF EXCRUTIATINGLY COMIC OVERTONES!').[76] The lengths that the pressbook goes to in order to stress the accessibility of this production reflect a concern that the film would indeed be perceived as too highbrow and too British.

The idea that Bergner's foreign accent would appeal to a global audience could not be more misguided – it is hard to imagine a more unlikable Rosalind. She bellows out her lines incomprehensibly and in the guise of Ganymede irritatingly waves a duster-shaped twig at everyone she encounters. Her performance is excessively theatrical, as if she is speaking to a huge audience with gestures to match. The immaculately dressed forest party seem not to lack in any comfort and thus it is no surprise that so many arrive for the lavish wedding party at the end. Olivier, perhaps unwittingly, upstages Bergner (even

---

[73] Bergner's 'Rosalind' Her Best-Loved Role', *As You Like It*, Pressbook, 1936, 14.
[74] '*As You Like It*, Grandest Fun Ever Brought to Screen', Ibid., 15.
[75] 'So you *think* you don't like Shakespeare?', Ibid., 11.
[76] Ibid., 11–12.

though he felt the film a failure)[77] but he also seems to keep at arm's length from her throughout, never allowing us to believe in a love story. Kenneth Rothwell disagrees, seeing in Olivier's performance 'a sullen pupil called on to read aloud in class'.[78] In truth, he does appear to distance himself from the role, even the poster image for the film shows him looking beyond Rosalind, a strange image to select for a romantic movie.

In spite of a treatment suggested by J.M. Barrie and a score by William Walton, the film is disappointing even compared to its American counterparts. Bergner's performance, rather than liberating the film from the difficulties of Shakespeare's language, magnifies its incomprehensibility. She may look the part, but she sounds dreadful. Among the survivors of this film are David Lean (the then young film editor), who went on successfully to direct adaptations of *Great Expectations* (1946), *Oliver Twist* (1948), *Doctor Zhivago* (1965) and *A Passage to India* (1984), and Laurence Olivier, who was to later become identified with cinematic Shakespeare, but who at this stage of his career, felt that Shakespeare and film did not mix, reminiscent perhaps of those in the late twenties and early thirties who were similarly cynical about the longevity of sound.[79] This view that Shakespeare was unfilmable prevailed into the next decade.

Hidden Shakespeare

The words of Shakespeare in this period did not flourish on screen but the stories found modernized counterparts that proved successful indeed. The rationale for choosing plays in the early sound period is easy to gauge: *The Taming of the Shrew* offers audiences entrance to the private life of a famous Hollywood couple, *A Midsummer Night's Dream* is a play allowing for a display of 'a galaxy of stars', *Romeo and Juliet* is a vehicle for George

---

[77] Crowl, 8.
[78] Kenneth Rothwell, *A History of Shakespeare on Screen: A Century of Film and Television* (Cambridge: Cambridge University Press, 1999), 50.
[79] See Crowl, 8 and John Cottrell, *Laurence Olivier* (Upper Saddle River, NJ: Prentice-Hall, 1975), 101–3.

Cukor who became renowned for making films appealing to women and *As You Like It* can be seen as exploiting the success of the screwball, romantic comedy genre. But try as they did, these movies did not succeed so well as the films which employed Shakespearean plots without the words, such as the gangster films which, like *Richard III* or *Macbeth*, gave eloquence to the criminal mind, or the romantic comedies such as multi-award winning *It Happened One Night* (1934), directed by Frank Capra and starring Claudette Colbert and Clark Gable. The film begins with a story resembling *Romeo and Juliet* (a father preventing his daughter from marrying the man of her choice) and ends, like *Much Ado About Nothing* with a couple married in spite of their initial contempt for each other and with the full backing of the bride's father. Colbert's character undergoes a series of humiliations, including food deprivation and a spanking, recalling, above all, *The Taming of the Shrew*. Perhaps the most successful 'non' Shakespearean Shakespeare films of this period are the biopics, *The Private Life of Henry VIII* (Korda, 1933) and *Cleopatra* (DeMille, 1934). Both movies have escaped scrutiny by Shakespeare film critics, perhaps due to their flaunting of the differences between Shakespeare's language and that spoken in 1930s popular cinema. While *Cleopatra*, starring Claudette Colbert, roughly follows the storyline of both *Julius Caesar* and *Antony and Cleopatra*, its verbal departure from Shakespeare is peculiarly observed in reviews. In *The New York Times*, Mordaunt Hall implicitly dismisses it as not Shakespearean (as if viewers are expecting some Shakespeare): 'There are moments when the dialogue is reminiscent of the Shakespearean speech and other occasions when it is so modern that one almost expects Mighty Caesar to have a typewriter and telephone at his elbow.'[80] It is revealing, however, that the only vaguely potentially Shakespearean films are successful – both *The Private Life of Henry VIII* (1933) and *Cleopatra* (1934) were box office successes and Academy Award winners – because they are only vaguely or potentially, but not quite Shakespearean.[81]

---

[80] *The New York Times*, 17/08/34, http://www.nytimes.com/movie/review?_r=1&res=9A0DE5D8133C E23ABC4F52DFBE66838F629EDE (Accessed 12/09/14).

[81] Charles Laughton received the Oscar for Best Actor (1934). *Cleopatra* was nominated for 'Best Picture', 'Best Sound, Recording', 'Best Film Editing', Best Assistant Director' and won for 'Best cinematography' (1935). See Chapter 5.

But we enter here into the game of determining when is an adaptation not an adaptation and certainly these films were not applauded in relation to their potential Shakespearean origins, in fact as Louis B. Mayer famously proclaimed, the name of Shakespeare is best not mentioned at all. But what is significant is that in this period Shakespeare was a commercial flop and that Shakespeare films could not be regarded as such unless they contained the words of the playwright.

The latter requirement seems to have filtered into a general conception of adaptation, without it ever being explicitly stated: to qualify as an adaptation, authorial words must be spoken. That Shakespeare films begin in the sound period seems to be a notion generally accepted. Even Graham Greene, initially an opponent of sound, in his reviews of these films counts them as the only movies to date that adapt Shakespeare. How soon the past is forgotten![82] In the field of Shakespeare adaptations, the introduction of sound results in a (at least temporary) cultural forgetfulness of all the silent adaptations of Shakespeare's plays with an emerging assumption that it is the words, and the words alone, that matter.

These talkie adaptations of Shakespeare's plays were marketed for both their retention of Shakespeare's words (making them the 'first' adaptations of the plays) and their global appeal, special selling points which were, in hindsight, a contradiction in terms. Words were indeed both requisites and poison for the translation of Shakespeare to screen, and these contradictory requirements would haunt the entire field of adaptation studies for most of the twentieth century. While continuing to claim film's pedagogical potential, Shakespeare's cultural capital was not worth a lot and film-makers needed to look at 'lesser' writers for source material. In this early era of sound film, Shakespeare was at his best when either silent or forgotten.

---

[82] In his review of *Romeo and Juliet*, Graham Greene writes of this fourth attempt to screen *Shakespeare* (following *The Taming of the Shrew, A Midsummer Night's Dream* and *As You Like It*). *The Spectator*, 23/10/1936, in *The Pleasure Dome: The Collected Film Criticism 1935–40*, ed. John Russell Taylor (London: Secker & Warburg, 1972), 109–11, 109.

3

Sound Dickens

The marketing of Dickens adaptations followed a similar pattern to that of Shakespeare, with the exception that this time it seems to have been successful. Just as in the case of Shakespeare films of this period, sound – in particular the spoken word – was fetishized in promotional materials of 'talkie' adaptations of Dickens's novels, positioning the films, in defiance of their numerous silent predecessors, as the *first* adaptations of the author's work. These films, spanning the period 1929–35, are regarded in this chapter as victims of their own successes, largely forgotten in our cultural memories and in critical regard due to the perceived superiority of their predecessors, while, at the same time, creating a 'brand' of adaptation for later films to emulate. This chapter considers the branding of adaptations of Dickens's novels in the sound era, in particular, MGM's 1935 blockbusters, *David Copperfield* (directed by George Cukor and adapted by Hugh Walpole, Howard Eastabrook and Lenore J. Coffee) and *A Tale of Two Cities* (directed by Jack Conway with a screenplay by W.P. Lipscomb and S.N. Behrman) in relation to the employment of sound, both in promotional activities and in the films themselves.

Advertising in the 1930s, in certain literary circles, was regarded as a decay of language, a levelling down in which the good life is measured in materialistic terms and representing just how far writers were prepared to sink in order to sell a product.[1] The view that money and art cannot mix has stigmatized literary and film studies, a prejudice perhaps that accounts for why the literature of advertising has been so overlooked in literary studies, in particular. This chapter, through the use of pressbooks, trailers and other

---

[1] See Leavis and Thompson, and Chapter 1, section titled 'Literary opposition'.

promotional materials, considers the advertising of Dickens in relation to adaptations of his novels in the sound era. The tactics employed to market these films largely consist of an insistence on the films' literary credentials and historical veracity through their use of the spoken word. Indeed the heavy-handed promotional apparatus seems to have succeeded in drawing in the public while disguising the fact that the films themselves seem to resist the wordiness that the advertisers boast.

The more we look at these films as products of the sound era, the more it becomes clear that sound is far from taken for granted at the time of their production (as it is today) and through the marketing and in the films themselves, at least two distinct audiences are appealed to: those who eagerly await to hear Dickens spoken for the first time on screen and those who prefer to see rather than hear the novels. This dual approach to sound creates a brand of Dickens film, still prevalent today. This chapter regards these adaptations of Dickens as 'Dickens talkies', films which are self-consciously aware of themselves as speaking Dickens's words on screen for the first time and within a period in which sound was both celebrated and lamented.

But why adapt Dickens at all? There must be good reasons why Dickens has been filmed, year in year out, since the inception of cinema. What was it about his work that led so many filmmakers to translate it from the very beginning of cinema? Firstly, like Shakespeare, Dickens was himself an adaptor; we can trace characters, events and expressions in his fiction to a wide range of earlier sources. In *Nicholas Nickleby*, the central figure is a Victorian version of an Elizabethan/Jacobean revenger who temporarily works as an actor and adaptor, a nod to Dickens's own position, attentive to a demanding audience and to particularly taxing critics:

> Profiting by these and other lessons, which were the result of the personal experience of the two actors, Nicholas willingly gave them the best breakfast he could, and when he at length got rid of them, applied himself to his task, by no means displeased to find that it was so much easier than he had at first supposed ...
>
> 'I hope you have preserved the unities, sir?' said Mr Curdle. 'The original piece is a French one,' said Nicholas. 'There is abundance of incident, sprightly dialogue, strongly-marked characters–'

'–All unavailing without a strict observance of the unities, sir,' returned Mr Curdle. 'The unities of the drama, before everything.'

'Might I ask you,' said Nicholas, hesitating between the respect he ought to assume, and his love of the whimsical, 'might I ask you what the unities are?'[2]

Secondly, many critics have pointed to Dickens's cinematic style of writing famously observed by Sergei Eisenstein in his 1944 essay, 'Dickens, Griffith, and the Film Today' in which he declares Dickens a prophet of the narrative film to come, especially in his use of parallel plotting or montage, descriptive details, such as close-up, and his synoptic cityscapes.[3] His so-called filmic style then goes some way to explaining the appeal of Dickens to the silent screen. Dickens's writing is often dreamlike and magical and *A Christmas Carol*, in particular, offered early film-makers opportunities to show off special effects, such as in the presentation of ghosts.

Thirdly, Dickens pictorial writing is also reflected in the illustrations of his novels that have been regarded as providing a template for early film adaptations of his work, described by Michael Eaton as 'animated illustrations.'[4] Kamilla Elliott looks at silent adaptations of Dickens and challenges 'The myth of the cinematic novel [which], intriguingly, asserts that film grew out of the Victorian novel – though not from its words and not from its illustrations.'[5] Elliott argues that in the late silent period, film language does not only replace verbal language but there is also 'a complex interweaving of intertitles and scene shots to form verbal-visual "sentences",'[6] possibly laying the groundwork for the incorporation of spoken words in adaptations in the sound era. In other words, illustrations and words, or a strategic manipulation of Victorian iconography, are essential to Dickens's translation to screen.

If the number of films produced based on an author's work is a measure of canonicity, then Dickens in the silent period of cinema was a close second to

[2] *Nicholas Nickelby*, ed. Michael Slater (Harmondsworth, Middlesex: Penguin, 1981), 376–86.
[3] See Garrett Stewart, 'Dickens, Eisenstein, film', in *Dickens on Screen*, ed. John Glavin (Cambridge: Cambridge University Press, 2003), 122–44 and Grahame Smith, *Dickens and the Dream of Cinema* (Manchester: Manchester University Press, 2003).
[4] http://www.screenonline.org.uk/tours/dickens/tour3.html, accessed 29/04/12.
[5] 'Cinematic Dickens and Uncinematic Words', in *Dickens on Screen*, ed. John Glavin (Cambridge: Cambridge University Press, 2003), 113–21, 115.
[6] Ibid., 119.

Shakespeare. As one very conservative measure, Denis Gifford lists seventy-five Shakespeare adaptations in the first 19 years of motion pictures while the count for Dickens is sixty.[7] In the earliest days of cinema, Dickens was adapted in short films including *The Death of Nancy Sykes* (1897), *Mr Bumble the Beadle* (1898) and *Scrooge; or Marley's Ghost* (1901) and the recently uncovered *The Death of Poor Jo* (1901); and his narratives continued to be adapted throughout the silent period. Today Jane Austen equals Dickens as the most adaptable of nineteenth-century authors, but in the silent period her novels were overlooked by the film industry, possibly because they were too static in terms of location, too reliant on conversations and lacking in grand narratives, like those of both Shakespeare and Dickens, stories familiar enough to be portrayed visually. But in the early sound period, Austen was still overlooked by film-makers and Dickens substantially overtook Shakespeare in the number of English-speaking adaptations. This chapter attempts to redress the critical neglect of these films in Dickens and adaptations scholarship, offering some explanation as to why Dickens's writing was so adaptable to early sound cinema. It contextualizes these adaptations of Dickens's novels in relation to the new sound era by surveying the movies themselves and through an analysis of the lengths that the promoters of these films went to in order to call attention to 'the new sound' of Dickens.

A group of Dickens's adaptations almost entirely passed over in film and adaptation criticism is the early sound films, produced at a time when the new technology was still in an experimental form, when actors were making the uncertain transition from silent to speaking parts and when cineastes and literary critics were dismissive of the new technology, either seeing sound as throwing film back to a reliance on theatre (and threatening film's status as art) or producing a diluted and potentially dangerous product, an 'impure cinema' (an unhealthy mixture of film and literature),[8] likened to an 'opiate' by William Hunter in the first issue of the literary journal, *Scrutiny.*[9] Although

---

[7] *Books and Plays in Films 1896–1915* (London: McFarland, 1991).

[8] See Deborah Cartmell and Imelda Whelehan, *Screen Adaptation: Impure Cinema* (Basingstoke: Palgrave, 2010), 127–31.

[9] See William Hunter, 'The Art-Form of Democracy?', *Scrutiny* 1:1 (1932): 61–5 (62).

a few of these films have received considerable attention, in particular, *David Copperfield* (1935, directed by George Cukor), these films need to be read together, within the context of the new 'talkies' and the audience's sense of wonderment that they were hearing as well as seeing Dickens on film for the first time. They also need to be regarded within a period in which writers, such as Aldous Huxley and Graham Greene, were hopeful that sound would never catch on.[10] As David Gomery has argued, 'the speed of sound' was something of a myth, with some audiences in the 1930s still nostalgic for the silent past.[11] In a radio broadcast of 1937, entitled 'The Cinema', Graham Greene reflects on his initial disdain for and his still lingering reservations concerning the talkies:

> There was a time when many of us thought the talkies were going to be the end of cinema .... The trouble with most films now is that they pay lip service to life. People talk, you see, and that's like life: soon they will be coloured and that's a bit more like life: and then they will be stereoscopic. But somehow life as we know it seeps away – and what's left is neither fish nor fowl. We look in vain for pictures with a real appeal to the huge audiences of the cinema, for a Dickens of the screen.[12]

The 'Dickens of the screen' that Greene longed for in 1937 was clearly not the recent Dickens adaptations of the early sound period, which deserve no mention in this broadcast but for films that emulate Dickens's mixture of mass appeal and cultural value: for film to be 'the new Dickens'. Nonetheless, Greene's desire for a combination of art, prestige and popularity on screen (akin to Dickens on the page) was something that the creators and promoters of these adaptations of Dickens in the early sound period also yearned to accomplish. We have to regard these adaptations of the late 1920s and early 1930s, in the wake of *The Jazz Singer* (1927), as charting new ground, combining a successful and tested product (Dickens translated to screen) with a new and controversial addition: words. And in the publicity materials these

---

[10] For an example of a violent attack on the new talkie, see Aldous Huxley, 'Silence Is Golden' (1929), in *Authors on Film*, ed. Harry M. Geduld (Bloomington, IN: Indiana University Press, 1972), 68–74. See page 25 above.

[11] Douglas Gomery, *The Coming of Sound* (New York: Routledge, 2005).

[12] Graham Greene, 'The Cinema', Broadcast on the BBC National Service (29 August, 1937), in *Mornings in the Dark: The Graham Greene Film Reader*, ed. David Parkinson (Manchester: Carcanet, 1993), 511–4, 512.

films audaciously proclaim themselves not as continuing a long-standing tradition of film adaptations of Dickens's novels but rather as initiators of a new tradition, the first ever, even the definitive adaptations of the novelist's work: a 'Dickens of the screen'.

If we compare major Shakespeare and Dickens adaptations in this period, then we can see how Dickens triumphs where Shakespeare fails in terms of box office success and sheer number of adaptations.

Dickens Adpations 1927–36	Shakespeare Adaptations 1927–36
The Only Way (Herbert Wilcox, *A Tale of Two Cities*, 1927)	*The Taming of the Shrew* (Pickford, 1929)
Scrooge (British Sound Productions, 1928)	*A Midsummer Night's Dream* (Warner Brothers', 1935)
Rich Man's Folly (*Dombey and Son*, Paramount, 1931)	*Romeo and Juliet* (MGM, 1936)
Oliver Twist (Monogram, 1933)	*As You Like It* (Inter-Allied, 1936)
Klein Dorrit (*Little Dorrit*, Bavaria Film, 1934)	
Great Expectations (Universal 1934)	
The Old Curiosity Shop (British International Pictures, 1934)	
David Copperfield (MGM 1935)	
Mystery of Edwin Drood (Universal 1935)	
Scrooge (Twickenham Film Studios 1935)	
A Tale of Two Cities (MGM 1935)	

Essentially, the Shakespeare 'talkies' were condemned as either too wordy or not wordy enough and after the experiments (and disappointing failures) of *The Taming of the Shrew*, *A Midsummer Night's Dream*, *Romeo and Juliet* and *As You Like It* (1929–36), it wasn't until *Henry V* in 1944 that another Shakespeare talkie was made and when filmed Shakespeare captured the public's imagination.[13] Compared to four Shakespeare films, there were eleven film adaptations of Dickens in the same period, including one silent and one

---

[13] As discussed in the previous chapter.

short. The first talkie adaptation of Dickens was *Scrooge*, starring Bransby Williams, made a year after *The Jazz Singer* when the new technology was very much in its infancy. Unfortunately, this film is lost, but it provides some evidence of the immediate appeal of Dickens's narratives to the new sound cinema.

Why did Dickens adapt so much easier to sound than Shakespeare? During the Great Depression and in the early days of the Production Code (released from 1930), film's much sought after respectability and the need to contest the perceived greed of a glamorous film industry was provided for in one fell swoop by Dickens. The period witnessed a 'DICKENS BOOM', as Guerric DeBona observes, as the novels provided cinema with narratives that are simultaneously escapist while reassuringly illustrative of how in the previous century people managed in even worse times.[14] The author's different voices also provided sound cinema with an opportunity to 'show off', in mockery of the rich, greedy and pretentious rather than the poor. Unfortunately, these Dickens talkies are overshadowed by their cinematic offspring, films such as David Lean's *Great Expectations* (1946) and *Oliver Twist* (1948) and Brian Desmond's *A Christmas Carol* (1951, starring Alastair Sim), films that usurped their predecessors, taking adaptations to new levels. But this period of Dickens adaptations does not deserve to be forgotten: these films were distinctly aware of themselves as charting new territory in the field of sound and the sheer number of them is testimony to their success. In the case of novel adaptations, sound meant 'spoken words', a feature that came to define what constituted what it was to be a literary adaptation (and correspondingly stifling the approach to film adaptations of literary texts to fruitless word counting exercises and/or quests for fidelity for most of the twentieth century).[15]

Almost all of these films, spanning the period of 1928–35, share certain generic features. They begin with a homage to the adapted novel, focusing

---

[14] Guerric DeBona, *Film Adaptation in the Hollywood Studio Era* (Urbana, IL: University of Chicago Press, 2010), 41.

[15] Attacks on adaptation 'fidelity criticism' (the 'not as good as the book' approach) are plentiful in the twenty-first century. See Robert Stam, 'Introduction: The Theory and Practice of Adaptation', in *Literature and Film: A Guide to the Theory and Practice of Film Adaptation*, ed. Robert Stam and Alessandra Raengo (Malden, MA and Oxford: Blackwell, 2005), 1–52, 14–16.

on the words of the titles and first pages of Dickens's volumes. They are set in period costume, use period music, especially Christmas music at the most sentimental sections of the story, and make extensive use of intertitles. Indeed most fit precisely into what Thomas Leitch has identified as the 'adaptation genre'.[16] Before looking at the two major productions of this period, *David Copperfield* (Cukor, 1935) and *A Tale of Two Cities* (Conway, 1935), a brief survey of the 'lesser' Dickens films of this period indicates just how easily Dickens was accommodated to the 'talkies'. Oddly, given the history of Dickens on screen, the first major adaptation of Dickens's (*Dombey and Son*) *Rich Man's Folly*, 1931, directed by John Cromwell for Paramount, does not conform to Leitch's 'adapatation genre' insofar as it is a contemporary reworking and seems to conceal its Dickensian roots. In the pressbook, there is only one mention of its origins in *Dombey and Son*,[17] suggesting anxieties about marketing the film as an adaptation in this early period of sound, a concern which vanishes two years later with the release of *Oliver Twist* (directed by Wiliam J. Cowen) which, seemingly oblivious to *Rich Man's Folly*, stridently advertises itself as 'the first sound film dealing with any of Dickens's world-famous novels'.[18]

In contrast to *Rich Man's Folly*, marketing of *Oliver Twist* (Pathe, William J. Cohen, 1933) is in terms of its Dickensian roots, including cultural value and inspirational charity, with suggestions to exhibitors such as to remind audiences that it is 'a literary masterpiece and an assigned text book in English courses' and if 'there is an orphan asylum in your locality, invite the inmates under the auspices of your leading local newspaper to a special morning show'.[19] The film was advertised in *The Dickensian* ('FOR ALL LOVERS OF DICKENS: A FAVOURITE DICKENS STORY COMES TO LIFE'), and praised by the journal's reviewer in spite of its numerous anachronisms; the speech, in particular, was applauded as being 'remarkably free from American

---

[16] Thomas Leitch, 'Adaptation, the Genre', *Adaptation* 1:2 (2008): 106–20. Features of the 'adaptation genre' are expanded by Christine Geraghty, 'Foregrounding the Media: *Atonement* (2007) as an Adaptation, *Adaptation* 2:2 (2009): 91–109 and Deborah Cartmell, '*Pride and Prejudice* and the Adaptation Genre', *Journal of Adaptation in Film & Performance* 3:3 (2010): 227–43.

[17] 'The story of "Rich Man's Folly" was suggested by the Charles Dickens classic "Dombey and Son".' *Rich Man's Folly*, Pressbook, 1931.

[18] *Oliver Twist*, Pressbook, 1933.

[19] Pressbook, 1933.

Figure 3.1 Cover of the Pressbook, *Oliver Twist* (Pathe, William J. Cohen, 1933)

accent'.[20] While there was one European adaptation of Dickens in this period, *Klein Dorrit* (*Little Dorrit*, Bavaria Film, directed by Carl Lamac, 1934), it is not surprising that all the other films are in English in the spirit of producing films that are 'faithful' to the novelist's words within the new sound era. *Great Expectations* released in 1934 by Universal Studios and directed by Stuart Walker is an adaptation now rarely seen due to the release of David Lean's adaptation over a decade later, an adaptation that trumps and, to an extent, obliterates the earlier film in the minds of audiences from 1946 onwards. Brian McFarlane notes how the film pales in comparison to following adaptations, intimating that it fully deserves its obscure place within the history of Dickens on screen, especially given that it only manages to retain the hinge points of Dickens's novel.[21] But it can be seen very much as a product of its period, very much aware of its audience; at a time in which the world is struggling out of Depression, the film suppresses Pip's upstart snobbery, perhaps a subject too close to home for an audience who will invariably recognize the film's

[20] '*OLIVER TWIST* FILMED AGAIN', *The Dickensian* 29: 4 (1933), 302.
[21] Brian McFarlane, 'Great Expectations (1934): A Hollywood Studio Romance', in *Screen Adaptations: Charles Dickens' 'Great Expectations': The Relationship Between Text and Film* (London: Methuen, 2008), 83–94.

stars as having experienced a similar trajectory to that of Pip: from rags to, what many regarded as undeserved, riches. A far cry from this sanitized *Great Expectations* is *The Old Curiosity Shop* (British International Pictures, 1934), directed by veteran Dickens director, Thomas Bentley, who together with Thomas Hepworth is credited by Joss Marsh as laying the foundation 'whereby Dickens = London = Victorian = England'.[22] Bentley made his name as a performer of Dickens's characters on stage and as an adaptor of Dickens in the silent period (which led to his acceptance in Hollywood). This, Bentley's third *Curiosity Shop*, is his first Dickens adaptation in the sound era and seems to be as much indebted to the horror tradition as it is to his commitment to a manufactured view of Dickensian England as it is dominated by an increasingly monstrous Quilp, sadistic and lascivious, played with gusto by Hay Petrie. Quilp, in classic horror fashion, gradually develops the accoutrements of the typical Hollywood monster, becoming increasingly unkempt and more hunched as the film progresses. The next Dickens adaptation of this period, Universal's *Mystery of Edwin Drood* (dir. Stuart Walker, 1935), is equally dark in tone, moving at breakneck pace with Claude Rains, playing the opium-addicted choirmaster, whose moodiness and murderous looks at those who displease him make him guilty long before he is predictably caught red-handed at the film's close. This more sinister side of Dickens is continued in *Scrooge*. Even the 2009 DVD cover of *Scrooge* (Twickenham Film Studios 1935, starring Seymour Hicks) identifies the film as 'The original Charles Dickens' classic tale of Scrooge', implying erroneously that this is the first ever screen adaptation of *A Christmas Carol*. While the level of production is low, unlike its slick American counterparts, it is worth pausing on the film's oscillation between silence and sound through the figure of the Ghost of Christmas Yet to Come. The shadow of a hand pointing calls attention to the power of images over words, creating a legacy for all the *Christmas Carol*s to follow.

While the film is a reworking of earlier versions (using the already 'tried and tested' Seymour Hicks who had appeared as Scrooge in numerous stage performances and in a film produced in 1913), the triumph of silence over

---

[22] Joss Marsh, 'Dickens and film', in *The Cambridge Companion to Charles Dickens*, ed. John O. Jordan (Cambridge: Cambridge University Press, 2001), 204–29, 207.

Figure 3.2 *Scrooge* (Twickenham Film Studios, Henry Edwards, 1935)

sound is striking in the new talkie adaptation of this perennial Christmas favourite.[23] The silent pointing shadow of the Ghost of Christmas Yet to Come is simultaneously the most frightening and most eloquent character in this early sound film. As Malcolm Andrews has noted, it is indeed ironic that the 'Future' is seen as silent within the context of the new sound era.[24] MGM produced two adaptations of Dickens within this period, *David Copperfield* and *A Tale of Two Cities*; and while promoters eagerly proclaimed the advantages of sound, the films themselves are arguably at their best, like this *Scrooge*, when silent.

The Dickens flagship film of this period, *David Copperfield*, directed by George Cukor, and produced by David. O. Selznick at MGM in 1935, boasts its literary credentials through its screenwriter, the popular, middle-brow writer and Chairman of The Book Society, Hugh Walpole. Star power rather than literary power produced financial results in this period, as Guerric DeBona

---

[23] See Graham Petrie, 'Silent Film Adaptations of Dickens: Part II: 1912–1919', *The Dickensian* 97:2 (2001): 101–15, and 'Silent Film Adaptations of Dickens: Part II: 1920–1927, *The Dickensian* 97:3(2001): 197–214.

[24] I am grateful to Malcolm Andrews, editor of *The Dickensian*, for his helpful comments on this chapter.

has demonstrated, but for this adaptation, the 'Drawings by Phiz' seem to have dictated casting decisions.[25] Indeed the actors are introduced in the opening credits framed in books as if they are characters on the original pages.

Figure 3.3 Opening Credits of *David Copperfield* (MGM, George Cukor, 1935)

The film capitalizes on the appeal of 'waifs' during the Depression (as demonstrated by Shirley Temple's ever rising star in this period)[26] when the plight of children had an immediate relevance, but Freddie Bartholomew's sentimental performance as young David is offset by W.C. Fields's Micawber, both affected by and disinterested in the plight of his lodger. The film was a huge box office success, both in the US and abroad, grossing just under $3 million in its eighty-six-week run[27] but, I suggest, not so popular with academics and film critics, as revealed by *The Dickensian*'s qualms 'That English masterpieces should be left in the hands of American film producers was unthinkable'[28] and while reviewing it favourably, the journal is quick to point out that 'literary and discriminating reviewers have raised doubts as

---

[25] *Film Adaptation in the Hollywood Studio Era*, 43, 53. *Alice in Wonderland* (1933) made a similar decision, but used John Tenniel's illustrations for costume designs which had the unfortunate result of hiding the stars of this production. See Chapter 6.

[26] See Chapter 6.

[27] Thomas Schatz, *The Genius of the System: Hollywood Film-making in the Studio Era* (London: Random House, 1998), 169.

[28] Walter Dexter, 'Review of *David Copperfield*', *The Dickensian* 30:3 (1934), 159.

to the propriety of filming "Dickens." [29] Graham Greene makes a scathing reference to it in *Brighton Rock*[30] and makes no secret of his distaste for middle-brow writer Hugh Walpole (co-screenwriter), who he groups with J.B. Priestley: both 'rather crude minds representing no more of contemporary life than is to be got out of a holiday snapshot'.[31] Greene's disdain for Walpole is shared by the British literati, most prominently, the Leavises, somehow threatened by the novelist's popularity and at pains to demonstrate that such writing (especially by those who sink to the depths of screenwriting) cannot stand beside the 'classics'.[32]

Untouched by British critics' opposition to Walpole as opportunistic and shallow, MGM present him as a literary genius. The trailer to the production begins with Walpole himself (reverentially introduced as a literary giant by Lionel Barrymore) who enthuses about his role in the film, claiming 'It's certainly an honour to be connected with putting *David Copperfield* on to the screen for the first time in history'.[33]

Walpole (who even has a small part in the film as a vicar) repeats his endorsement on a radio promotion for the film where he is introduced as a world authority on Dickens. The film's pressbook also stresses Walpole's involvement in the production and revels in the novelist's appreciation of the demanding role of screenwriter, cheekily implying that screenwriting exceeds the challenges of novel writing. The first page prominently features a letter allegedly from Walpole written to David O. Selznick:

> I can't leave Hollywood without telling you how pleased I am with the "DAVID COPPERFIELD" picture. I know that Dickens, if he could see the film would be proud.[34]

---

[29] '"DAVID COPPERFIELD" ON THE SCREEN', *The Dickensian* 31:3 (1935), 223–5, 223.

[30] In *Brighton Rock* (1938), Ida Arnold is seen as over-sentimental and mocked for crying over the film of *David Copperfield* (London: Lightning Source, 2011; first published 1938), 29.

[31] Graham Greene in 'Subjects and Stories', in *Mornings in the Dark: The Graham Greene Film Reader*, ed. David Parkinson (Manchester: Carcanet, 2007), 409.

[32] Referring to Walpole as a simple crowd-pleaser was one thing that Greene had in common with the Leavises, who regarded a liking for Walpole's writing as synonymous with bad taste. F.R. Leavis refers to it as 'uplift' writing, the lowest form of commercial writing. See 'Mass Civilisation and Minority Culture', 1930, in *Education & the University* (London: Chatto & Windus, 1948), 160–1 and Q.D. Leavis, *Fiction and the Reading Public* (1932; London: Random House, 2000), 76.

[33] The trailer and radio promotion are available on the 2007 Tunrer Entertainment Co. and Warner Bros. Entertainment Inc. DVD.

[34] *David Copperfield*, Pressbook, 1935.

Figure 3.4 Hugh Walpole in Trailer for *David Copperfield* (MGM, George Cukor, 1935)

Typical of adaptations of this vintage, the film boasts its literary credentials and is identified as a first in spite of numerous silent precursors. The screenwriters are prominent in the pressbook, with Walpole repeatedly mentioned and co-screenwriter Howard Estabrook contributing an article that opens with the old chestnut: 'If Dickens were writing in Hollywood today, he would be the greatest screen dramatist of the hour. He would write more hit parts, create more new stars, and score more all-around box office success than any other writer!'[35] Included in the pressbook are actual pages from the novel, illustrated with stills from the film, demonstrating the closeness of the movie to Dickens's novel; indeed the integration of film pictures into the novel's pages implies the film's mise en scène enlarges on the novel's own illustrations. Historical veracity is also defended through the use of sound. Director George Cukor explains that sounds had to be reproduced 'exactly as they were in Dickens' time', a claim expounded in an article entitled 'The Cries of London':

---

[35] Howard Estabrook, 'What Dickens would Do to Hollywood', *David Copperfield*, Pressbook, 1934.

Noises that haven't been heard for at least half a century are faithfully reproduced in this film. The tapping of steel-shod canes on cobblestones; the rattling of iron-tyred wheels on granite blocks; the cheery salute of the tally-ho horns; the jingling of harness and the screaming of drivers who have been silenced three generations – all these things are revived on the screen.[36]

This film of *David Copperfield* is hailed as the first ever adaptation of Dickens's novel and marketed for its close attention to the book, sensitively rendered by a novelist who, at the time, is equated to Dickens in his contemporary stature. The publicity materials also brag about the authenticity of sound, distinguishing the film as an adaptation of the sound era: in other words, 'a first'.

Nonetheless, for a talkie, the film is noticeably quiet. It is punctuated by prolonged wordless sequences including Betsey's journey to the Copperfield home, David's long walk to Dover (lasting approximately three minutes without a single word spoken) and the drowning of Steerforth and Ham (the two minute silent sequence culminates in the reaction shots of David, speechless upon witnessing the dead Ham and Steerforth). While accompanied by non-diegetic music, these sequences would be very much at home in a silent film. The film's opening recalls its silent past, seen from Betsey's point of view. The camera follows her approach to the home of the Copperfields on a cold and windy night, accompanies her while she peers through the window at a weeping Clara caressing a cushion embroidered with 'BLESS THE BABY', while mouthing and gesturing at the window to be let in.

Audiences are kept in the silent mode in the opening sequence and kept waiting for the first words spoken by Betsey which initiate the film as the first 'talkie' adaptation of the novel: 'David Copperfield'. It is tempting to read the seemingly gratuitous decision to give Betsey earplugs while awaiting the birth of David (or rather, Betsey) as an insider joke, undermining the film's promotional materials' emphasis on sound.

---

[36] *David Copperfield*, Pressbook.

Figure 3.5 *David Copperfield* (MGM, George Cukor, 1935)

A Tale of Two Cities, directed by Jack Conway, MGM 1935, produced by David O. Selznick, released soon after *David Copperfield* is an adaptation, clearly capitalizing on the success of the earlier film. Including many of the cast of the previous MGM Dickens film (including Basil Rathbone, Edna May Oliver, Elizabeth Allen and Fay Chaldecott), it clearly markets itself on the earlier film's success with a suggested placard for exhibition: a signpost pointing to the film with the words 'Remember Copperfield'.[37] The publicity materials play up the film's ability to 'do' Dickens, with taglines, such as 'It will make thousands of Dickensians happy and new thousands of Dickensians',[38] and boasts that the film will go beyond mere pen and paper:

> [Dickens] needed no more material tools than pen, ink and paper. But to the motion picture makers, who had to bring these scenes to life upon the screen, there were problems which would completely confound a less competent industry.[39]

[37] *A Tale of Two Cities*, Pressbook, 1935.
[38] *A Tale of Two Cities*, Pressbook.
[39] Ibid.

Suggestions for advertising range from a book display with images from the film on the covers to a 'DICKENS CHARACTER WALKING THE STREETS', picturing a walking 'living book' with the film's poster image on the cover.

Figure 3.6 Pressbook, *A Tale of Two Cities*, Pressbook, 1935

The film is memorable for the extraordinary performance of Ronald Colman (who fought over the part with Leslie Howard), who makes a thoroughly convincing conversion from rake to saint. The other star of the film is the written word. Director Jack Conway pronounces the film's literary roots throughout, beginning with a bibliography in the title credits (*The French Revolution*, Thomas Carlyle, *Journal of the Temple*, M. Clery, *The Memoirs of Mlle. Des Echerolles* and *The Memoirs of M. Nicholas*) and in the opening shot of the famous first lines, cunningly revised to highlight the perceived role of this particular adaptation: 'IT was the best of times, it was the worst of times, it was the season of Light, it was the season of Darkness, we had everything before us, we had nothing before us ... in short, it was a period very like the present ... '.[40] Clearly 'the present' here is 1935 not 1859. Taking his cue from the film's introduction, Jason Stevens reads the film as responding to the issues confronting America in 1935: 'Within its first few seconds, MGM's A *Tale of Two Cities* invites a parallel between 1785 and New Deal-era America in the process of recovering from its crisis of authority'.[41] The film for Stevens was 'calculated to fully engage and discipline an angry populism before it could swerve to the far Right or the far Left'.[42] Without doubt, the film presents a warning regarding such popular insurrections, but it also creates a mood of nostalgia. With an overlapping cast and similar advertising strategies to *David Copperfield*, the later film seems to be even more rooted in its silent past.

For a talkie as late as 1935, intertitles seemingly needlessly play a major part throughout the film, as Allardyce Nicoll complained the year after the film's release, these seem backward looking in the new era of sound.[43] Intertitles are most prominently used when Madame Defarge, after witnessing the barbaric trampling of the innocent citizens, asks the question: 'Why?'. This sequence, as Charles Barr notes, which was given to a separate film unit and is reminiscent of the street demonstrations and police massacre of the silent masterpiece, *Battleship Potemkin* (Sergei M. Eisenstein, 1925), changes the mood of the film, from the personal to the political and from sound to silence.[44] As in the opening sequence of *David Copperfield*, the original audience, still very much in awe of the new 'talkie' pictures, must have been keenly aware

---

[40] This is a direct transcription from the film, including the ellipses.

[41] Jason Stevens, 'Insurrection and Depression-Era Politics in Selznick's *A Tale of Two Cities*, *Literature/ Film Quarterly* 34:3 (2006): 176–93, 176.

[42] Ibid., 178.

[43] See Chapter 1, note 9.

[44] See Charles Barr, 'Two Cities, Two Films', in *Charles Dickens, A Tale of Two Cities and the French Revolution*, ed. Colin Jones, Josephine McDonagh and Jon Mee (Houndmills: Palgrave, 2009), 166–87, 170. This shift in tone was not to the liking of A. Stewart Mason who reviewed the film for *The Dickensian*: 'Here there was too much realism and too little left to the imagination'. 'THE FILM OF A TALE OF TWO CITIES', *The Dickensian* 32: 3 (1936): 172.

of this reminder of cinema's silent past. Barr surmises that this probably is the unnamed sequence cut by the British Board of Film Censors due to its revolutionary content, especially its representation of the power of the mob, a dangerous message for an impressionable audience in the uncertainty of the pre-war period. The change of mood is also achieved by a stylistic shift from sound to silence. The word 'WHY?' leaves Madame Defarge's mouth and takes on a life of its own, translated to animated intertitle, superimposed and repeated in increasing size and corresponding exclamatory impact on the screen against shots of suffering.

Figure 3.7 *A Tale of Two Cities* (MGM, Jack Conway, 1935)

The word 'WHY', looking strangely like words such as 'POW', 'WHAM', 'SMASH' in comic-book adaptations, such as those popularized in the 1960s televised *Batman*, is repeated on screen before the intertitles change into increasingly cruel responses to the outrage, among them 'DEATH TO THEIR FRIENDS', 'DEATH TO THEIR SERVANTS', 'DEATH TO THE INNOCENT AS WELL AS THE GUILTY'. The transformation of the words on screen, from the initial repeated innocent question ('WHY?') into a series of vengeful responses, mirrors the transformation portrayed in the novel from innocence to experience: the revolutionaries' metamorphoses from victims to victimizers (and inverted in Sydney Carton's personal transformation from sinner to saviour).

Words – both written and spoken – play a key role in this film. They serve to remind the audience of cinema's silent past and function as silent witnesses; for instance in the Manette's Paris residence, Lucie and Sydney's conversation is silently underlined by a framed embroidery situated behind them featuring the words, 'I am the Resurrection and the Life' (a passage which, in the novel, Sydney remembers as having been spoken at his father's funeral). The embroidered words recall the silent past, when words were seen rather than heard.

Figure 3.8 *A Tale of Two Cities* (MGM, Jack Conway, 1935)

Dickens's words are spoken, the Bible's are seen. The film ends with the execution of Carton after which we hear his voice-over against a calm sky (presumably from Heaven) speaking the famous lines: 'It's a far, far better thing that I do than I've ever done; it is a far, far better rest that I go to, than I have ever known.' The film concludes abruptly with Dickens's words spoken by a disembodied voice followed by the intertitle, 'I am the Resurrection and the Life: he that believeth in me, though he were dead yet shall he live.' Once again, Dickens's spoken words are juxtaposed with the seen words of the Bible.

Although not as successful as *David Copperfield* in the box office,[45] this film, in my view is the best of the Dickens films in this period, especially in its visual use of words. The emphasis on words, both spoken and visualized, reflects the film's position within the new age of the 'talkie', which lovingly looks back to film's silent past, which in the final sequence is virtually 'sanctified' through its association with the Bible. This talkie is clearly not content to just reproduce the author's words so that we can hear them, but it also, to quote Joseph Conrad in his Preface to *The Nigger of the 'Narcissus'* (1897), is keen 'to make you hear, to make you feel – it is, before all, to make you *see*'.[46] The message of this extraordinary *Tale of Two Cities* seems to be that we can only read – or understand – a film, if we can both hear and see the words.

Unlike the publicity surrounding these films, which is so keen to call attention to the newfangled sound together with the literary prestige of Dickens, these adaptations have not forgotten their silent past and through a cunning manipulation of words and images, silence and sound, they look backwards as much as forwards, providing something not far from what Greene called a 'Dickens of the screen'.[47] In hindsight, the frantic attempts of the publicists to promote the films' literary pedigrees were misleading and possibly unnecessary. Dickens's writing was appealing to early sound cinema because it championed the poor and the downtrodden during the Depression Era, and the novels were still considered popular, so unlike Shakespeare adaptations (where the newly spoken words proved to be too many for the 'general fans' and too few for the literati),[48] the words were neither considered threatening to the audience nor demeaning to the author. The Dickens adaptations of this period are victims of their success: they created a 'Dickens screen brand' for films to follow and demonstrated that Dickens's words translated to film could appeal to a wide audience (so long as they continued to build upon their previous silent visual cinematic associations)

---

[45] Compared to *David Copperfield*'s 3 million, *A Tale of Two Cities* grossed 2.4 million (Schatz, 167).

[46] Joseph Conrad, Preface, in *The Nigger of the 'Narcissus': A Tale of the Sea* (London: John Grant, 1925), x.

[47] See note 7.

[48] See note 8.

and as such these pioneering early sound films were doomed to be overtaken and overshadowed by new generations of screen adaptations of Dickens's novels. Essentially, with few exceptions, the marketing of the films combined with the movies themselves provided a Dickens brand of films (unlike early Shakespeare talkies, a genre which had to be reinvented in the 1940s) that could be emulated again and again.

4

Gothic Adaptations

'Sell It for Its Horror': 1931 Gothic/Horror Adaptations and the Victory of the Shadow

Gothic adaptation of this period is unique insofar as while it identifies itself as adaptation in its publicity materials, it ultimately becomes associated with its additions to the literary hypotexts (to borrow Gérard Genette's term),[1] so much so that for most of the twentieth century, these films became what Disney films sought to become, the originals in the minds of their audiences. These adaptations succeed by becoming 'not adaptations', popular films, in the cinematic horror genre, in which in spite of their stories' literary origins, are accepted into the canon of classic cinema, reflecting what seems an explicit prioritizing of cinema over literature. In the early literature surrounding them, they hovered around identifying themselves as both 'adaptation' and 'horror'. But, as this chapter will indicate, the decision to put horror first was ultimately the right one. In order to succeed as both commercial and classic cinema, it was necessary to put genre first. This chapter will read three films released in 1931, *Dracula, Frankenstein* and *Dr. Jekyll and Mr. Hyde*, not in terms of horror and their contribution to that genre, but (as what is often forgotten) as adaptations, both through the paratextual materials and through the meta-adaptive images of mirrors and shadows, so prominent in all three films.

Julie Sanders identifies two types of literary 'borrowing': adaptation and appropriation. For Sanders, adaptation can be distinguished from appropriation insofar as it positions itself as an adaptation, by making explicit

---

[1] Gérard Gennette, *Palimpsests*, trans. Channa Newman and Claude Doubinsky (Lincoln, NE and London: University of Nebraska Press, 1997).

reference to the literary hypotext.[2] While it is not ultimately possible to distinguish 'adaptation' from 'appropriation' (as these terms assume that we can determine intentionality on the part of the film-makers), these adaptive strategies could be rewritten in terms of remembrance and forgetfulness, either intentional or unintentional, of the literary hypotext. Gothic adaptations can belong to both camps; certainly within the critical literature the fact that they are adaptations is often buried, forgotten or regarded as immaterial. But I would argue that in the early sound period, the films in both their marketing materials and in the films themselves very much position themselves as 'adaptations', copies, reflections or shadows of an 'original'.

While much has been written about the horror genre and the significance of these movies, surveying work on adaptations, these films are conspicuously absent, as if they are 1) too popular to be taken seriously within the field of adaptations or 2) too different in narrative from their literary hypotexts to be regarded as adaptations. Even into the new millennium, work on adaptation, even Robert Stam and Alessandra Raengo's much admired collections, largely consists of adaptations of canonical writers and on films that are best known as cinematic recreations of literary texts.[3] Writers on adaptation are more drawn to Kenneth Branagh's *Mary Shelley's Frankenstein* (1994) than to James Whale's movie, possibly due to the more reverential approach adopted by Branagh in what is undoubtedly an inferior film. In these films based on the novels by Shelley, Stoker and Stevenson, the genre of gothic turns into the less culturally esteemed 'horror'; while retaining hinge points of the gothic narratives, these films contribute to a new genre in which features not prominent in the literary hypotexts loom most large: mad scientists, deformed and mentally deranged sidekicks, dark steamy laboratories, dark winding staircases, a surreal and timeless landscape influenced by silent predecessors and German Expressionism, features which have become commonplace in what has become identified as the horror genre. David Skal goes so far as suggesting that 'horror films' were invented in 1931.[4]

---

[2] *Adaptation and Appropriation* (Abingdon, Oxon: Routledge, 2006).

[3] *A Companion to Literature and Film* (Malden, MA and Oxford: Blackwell, 2004), *Literature and Film: A Guide to the Theory and Practice of Film Adaptation* (Malden, MA and Oxford: Blackwell, 2005).

[4] David Skal, *The Monster Show: A Cultural History of Horror* (New York: Norton, 1993), 144.

As Kamilla Elliott has observed, most critics regard Mary Shelley's *Frankenstein*, Robert Louis Stevenson's *The Strange Case of Dr Jekyll and Mr Hyde* and Bram Stoker's *Dracula* as 'a foundational triptych for Gothic film adaptation' and most film scholars identify James Whale's *Frankenstein*, Tod Browning's *Dracula* and Rouben Mamoulian's *Dr. Jekyll and Mr. Hyde* 'as a foundational triptych from which they look both back to earlier Gothic films and forward to later ones'.[5] Elliott considers how gothic is often associated with parody in its critique of the *status quo* through the use of the supernatural, becoming an ideal vehicle for adaptation. For David Punter, 'Gothic has always sought to demonstrate to us … there [is] only distortion … what we see is always haunted by something else';[6] the genre is implicitly defined as a form of adaptation itself. These three films were all released in 1931, at the beginning of the sound era, and have become themselves 'classics', indeed 'originals' and as such parodied as much as or even more so than the literary texts from which they take their names. As has been noted,[7] influenced by German Expressionism, developed by a group of film-makers in the 1910s and 1920s (as epitomized by Robert Wiene's *The Cabinet of Dr Caligari*, 1920), these films are all preoccupied with casting shadows through chiaroscuro lighting effects and mirror reflections, the likes of which, while 'copies', are more frightening and more complex than the 'source' they reflect. These films, perhaps unknowingly, position themselves as adaptations by repeatedly calling attention to copies, sinister shadows, reflections and echoes, 'secondary' images that are more powerful and enduring than the source they seemingly emulate.

Marketing the 1931 horror films

The films, *Dracula*, *Frankenstein* and *Dr. Jekyll and Mr. Hyde*, all released in 1931, continue to be heralded as successful films within the gothic horror genre; and their marketing campaigns in their early days shamelessly placed

---

[5] 'Gothic-film-parody' *Adaptation* 1:1 (2008): 24–43, 24.
[6] David Punter, 'Introduction: The Ghost of a History', in *A New Companion to the Gothic*, ed. David Punter (Chichester: Wiley-Blackwell, 2012), 1–10, 3.
[7] Misha Kavka, 'Gothic on Screen', in *The Cambridge Companion to Gothic Fiction*, ed. Jerrold E. Hogle (Cambridge: Cambridge University Press, 2002), 209–28, 216.

genre at the forefront of their advertising. The pressbook for *Dracula* features numerous images and slogans, such as 'It isn't a show for the weak hearted or weak minded'.[8] In a double-bill with *Frankenstein*, suggestions for advertising included 'WE DARE YOU TO SEE: DRACULA AND FRANKENSTEIN' and 'FRANK and DRAC – THE HORROR BOYS – ARE AT IT AGAIN'.[9] Advertising suggestions appealed shamelessly to their audience's appetite for horror and the macabre, and even included the idea that a coffin and ambulance be placed outside the cinemas draped with the films' posters. But in addition to advertising the terrifying thrills experienced through these films, the intellectual benefits and the literary origins are not entirely swept aside. The pressbook for *Dracula* while briefly mentioning that 'Count Dracula is the principal character in Bram Stoker's story' also recommends 'a tie up … arranged with the psychology department at the University of California, Los Angeles. Instructors and students discussed the good or bad' 'of so called "horror".[10] *Frankenstein*'s literary pedigree is even more prominent in its pressbook. It advertises itself as 'Based Upon the Story By MARY WOLLSTONECRAFT SHELLEY' and incudes an article on 'a few facts about *Frankenstein*': 'To clear up one misapprehension, Frankenstein was the man who made the monster, and not the monster that somebody made.'[11] We are given details about Mary Shelley and a tie-up is recommended for local book dealers. 'Play up the book angle', we are told, 'It will pay you well. Make a large display of the book in your lobby.'[12] A sample of a newly designed Mary Shelley's *Frankenstein* is provided with the film poster on the cover and 'ILLUSTRATED WITH SCENES FROM THE UNIVERSAL PICTURE'.

The pressbook for *Dr. Jekyll and Mr. Hyde* explicitly advises exhibitors to 'sell it for its horror'. But while horror comes first, it is followed by 'the weird fantastic story' and 'third the top star names'.[13] In the pressbook, the film is seen in relation to the 'golden anniversary of the writing of Robert Louis Stevenson's horror classic' and features articles on the writing of the book referring to

---

[8]   Pressbook, 1931.
[9]   Ibid.
[10]   Ibid.
[11]   Ibid.
[12]   Ibid.
[13]   Ibid.

the film's predecessors, including the film of 1920, starring John Barrymore. The promoters also suggest advertising it through bookstore windows with a suggestion for a display 'built around a copy of the book … using other available thrillers and stills and posters of the picture. Suggested copy as follows: "The KING OF THEM ALL WHEN IT COMES TO HORROR THRILLS! … – SEE THE PICTURE – READ THESE THRILLERS".[14] Not only is the author given credit, but we learn, 'Robert Louis Stevenson, in person, acted a part in Paramount's version of the famous Robert Louis Stevenson classical story'. We read on to discover that it is the 'famous man's nephew' who 'plays a small supporting role in several of the scenes of the picture'.[15] Stevenson's presence is at the edges of the film, both in the marketing, title and production itself. Paramount, possibly unsure of the film's ultimate appeal, did not want to dismiss the film as a 'Prestige' production and its literary pedigree is part of its initial marketing strategy.

While clearly admitting that the selling point of these films is primarily 'horror', the pressbooks are keen to pursue the films' literary origins, seeing the books as helping to sell the films. However, unlike adaptations of Shakespeare and Dickens of this period, the books take a peripheral role in the marketing of the films, but a role nonetheless. It is possible that the films can be seen to succeed as adaptations because the book is of secondary importance, in both the production and their paratextual materials. What surprises me about the marketing of the films is the books' perseverance; but this is self-conscious and secondary to the demands of genre: 'horror comes first' then 'the weird fantastic story'. Unlike the marketing for Dickens and Shakespeare movies, the films' promotional materials do not ignore the silent past, and the spoken words of the author are explicitly of secondary importance.

These films, in particular, *Frankenstein*, have a distinguished critical and cultural heritage partially because genre and the acknowledgement of earlier films as precursory texts are privileged over literary adaptation. The marketing of the films does not exclude their literary heritage and the films themselves, I suggest, all make oblique reference to themselves as adaptations, through

[14] Ibid.
[15] Ibid.

literary inclusions and extensive use of mirrors and shadows, reflecting on themselves as reflections, adaptations of well-known stories.

Shadows and mirrors in *Dracula, Frankenstein* and *Dr. Jekyll and Mr. Hyde*

Appearing three months before the end of Hollywood's transition to sound film, *Dracula* directed by Tod Browning for Universal Studios, was available in three versions: one English, one Spanish and one silent and stands out for the performance in the English version of Bela Lugosi, with the first ever talking horror film initiating the 1930s horror cycle and Universal's association with the horror genre. Made during the Depression when the major studios were cutting costs, *Dracula* surprisingly provided Universal with a lifeline, culminating in $700,000, its largest profit in 1931, convincing the studio that horror sells.[16] A huge success in its own time, the film as Robert Spadoni notes, now seems somewhat creaky and disappointing, more cringe-inducing than horrifying. Spadoni considers this to be partially because a later audience has lost its wonderment in the novelty of sound: 'Did these moments register more strongly in 1931 than they do now in part because *Dracula*'s makers and first viewers all shared recent memories of watching sound films in which similar sensations had been aroused unintentionally?'[17] What is most memorable about the film, I argue, is not the novelty of sound but the nostalgia engendered by the silent sequences. In fact, as Spadoni observes the silence, robbed of live musical accompaniment, is even more silent than that to which audiences of the silent period had become accustomed.[18] The director, reputably uncomfortable with talkies, based the film on the play of 1924 by Hamilton Deane (revised for the American production by John L. Balderston in 1929) and for reasons of censorship was required to cut much of the content of the story, in particular the length it takes Lucy to die. Originally intended as a 'Prestige' production

---

[16] Mark A. Vieira, *Hollywood Horror: from Gothic to Cosmic* (New York: Harry N. Abrams, 2003), 35.

[17] Robert Spadoni, *Uncanny Bodies: The Coming of Sound Film and the Origins of the Horror Genre* (Berkeley, CA: University of California Press, 2007), 61.

[18] Ibid., 78.

(in a manner later to be adopted by MGM in such films as the 1935 *David Copperfield* and the use of the 'distinguished' writer, Hugh Walpole), Junior Laemmle of Universal commissioned Pulitzer Prize-winning novelist Louis Bromfield to write the screenplay. At first, an optimist of the potential of sound cinema, Bromfield's literary talents were ultimately unappreciated by Universal and as David J. Skal writes Bromfield 'disillusioned and drained with his encounter with *Dracula*, soon left Hollywood, never to return.'[19]

Indeed the progress of *Dracula's* script reveals a move away from 'literary adaptation' with the narrative transformed into something quite different from Bram Stoker's novel, initially for the sake of both economy of playing time and money. Rather than gesturing towards Stoker's 'New Woman', Mina is transformed into little more than a doll, recognizable now as female horror survivor, her behaviour completely regulated by the men in her life. Rather than Jonathan Harker, it is Renfield (played by Dwight Frye who becomes Fritz in *Frankenstein*) who visits Dracula's castle and as the film progresses, we see him become increasingly mad as he metamorphoses into the crooked and dishevelled figure associated with horror film villains; at the end literally a shadow of his former self. Lingering outside a closed door near the end of the film, his shadow reveals a monster about to pounce, a more accurate reflection of the real Renfield than presented by his actual diminutive and weak physical appearance (See Figure 4.1). The power of the shadow – or the monster lurking inside – is reinforced in Renfield's dismissal of Van Hesling a few seconds later, with a quotation from *Hamlet*: 'words, words, words';[20] indeed the images are infinitely more impressive than the words spoken in this early sound film.

The shadow, a stock feature of the silent 'Gothic' film becomes a prominent feature in Universal's later horror productions as does a lack of reverence for the words of the adapted texts. While Stoker's Dracula speaks perfect English, Bela Lugosi's charismatic Dracula is clearly 'foreign' and his eloquence is visual rather than verbal. The repulsive and articulate Dracula created by Stoker is transformed into a handsome figure, immaculately turned out in

---

[19] David J. Skal, *Hollywood Gothic: The Tangled Web of 'Dracula' from Novel to Stage to Screen* (1990; rev. New York: Faber, 2004), 175.

[20] *Hamlet* 2.2.195, *The Oxford Shakespeare: The Complete Works*, ed. John Jowett, William Montgomery, Gary Taylor and Stanley Wells.

Figure 4.1 *Dracula* (Universal, Tod Browning, 1931)

evening dress. As Cynthia Erb observes, this version 'is known for dispensing with the idea of Dracula as a grotesque creature'.[21] With a distinctive silk-lined cape and erect posture, he appears as an early version of Batman – in fact, the background to the opening credits of the film could be mistaken as from a contemporary *Batman* movie.

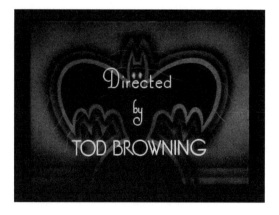

Figure 4.2 *Dracula* (Universal, Tod Browning, 1931)

---

[21] '1931: Movies and the Voice', in *American Cinema of the 1930s: Themes and Variations*, ed. Ina Rae Hark (New Brunswick: Rutgers University Press, 2007), 48–68, 53.

The film's roots in German Expressionism are immediately apparent through the cinematography of Karl Freund – his use of shadows, the fantastical architectural sets, jagged landscapes and the diagonal/vertical movement of the characters within the mise en scène, is reminiscent of Robert Wiene's acclaimed Expressionist film, *The Cabinet of Dr Caligari* (1920). An impressive staircase visualizes the descent into madness and death and the salvation of the good in the last sequence, with Dracula carrying Mina down the stairs quickly followed by Harker leading her upwards in the final frames of the film. This is an adaptation that is looking backwards rather than forward, with words taking secondary significance. The adaptation underplays itself as a talkie and through the reinvention of Dracula by Bela Lugosi (in spite of Universal's initial plan to cast Lon Chaney in the role and to stall the casting of Lugosi, regardless of his success on stage as Dracula), can be said, for many, to usurp Bram Stoker's novel as the 'definitive' version.

Identified as the top grossing film of 1931, *Frankenstein* is also, with *Jekyll and Hyde* and *Dracula*, normally placed in the top ten films of the year.[22] *Dracula's* success led to an immediate successor; and James Whale's *Frankenstein*, was an instantaneous success with rentals reaching $1.4 million by as early as 1932, creating for Universal a 'horror' franchise, as *Variety* announced: 'U Has Horror Cycle All to Self.'[23] Perhaps even more than any of the other horror adaptations of this period, *Frankenstein* is rarely devalued by critics with unhelpful comparisons to the novel upon which it is based. As Spadoni has observed, the film remains critically admired due to it being addressed to an audience who were more technologically aware having overcome their astonishment at the use of sound.[24] Much has been written about this film, but its identity as an adaptation is almost always forgotten or underplayed. From its earliest reception, the film is given a life independent of its 'creator', as the monster is separated from Frankenstein, and with the title role originally thought to be, right up until the film's release, played by Bela Lugosi, suggesting that this film will be as much an adaptation of Browning's

---

[22] See the IMDb for the most popular films released in 1931: http://www.imdb.com/year/1931/, Accessed 19/09/14.
[23] Quoted in Vieira, 41.
[24] Spadoni, 97.

film as Shelley's novel. Many of the ingredients are adapted from the earlier Universal film, including the set, with Edward Van Sloan revising his role as Van Helsing in Dr Waldman and Dwight Fry turning Renfield from *Dracula* into, Fritz, the hunchback assistant of Frankenstein.

In fact, a 1932 short film, *Boo*, directed by Albert DeMond and subtitled 'A Universal Brevity', makes the birth of *Frankenstein* from *Dracula* explicit through a comical account of what Frankenstein (using clips from the film) learns from Dracula (with clips from *Nosferatu*, starring Max Schreck, 1922), showing Boris Karloff's monster comically following Dracula around, observing his antics, a short that parodies what have already become clichés of the horror genre, with the dreamer protagonist, for instance, repeatedly going up and down a staircase, accompanied by a wisecracking narrator: 'but when he tries to go away he meets himself coming back. It looks as though he's having his ups and downs. He acts like Congress and always ends up where he started'.[25] *Boo* invites us to read the films not as adaptations of books, but as adaptations of films, with Boris Karloff's Frankenstein finding inspiration in Max Schreck's (strangely not Bela Lugosi's) Dracula.

Figure 4.3 *Boo* (Universal, Albert DeMond, 1932)

---

[25] The film is available on YouTube, http://www.youtube.com/watch?v=3tnuhSAjlRU, Accessed 19/09/14.

Frankenstein's adaptability and incitement to parody is again seen in Whale's own *Bride of Frankenstein*, released four years later. The 1935 film provocatively begins with Mary Godwin (played by Elsa Lanchester who also plays the Bride), Byron and Shelley, discussing *Frankenstein*, seemingly to remind or inform an audience of the film's literary origins as well as alluding to the author's unconventional or 'wayward' lifestyle, living with the poet, Percy Bysshe Shelley, while unmarried. The film resembles Mary Shelley's novel insofar as the monster is given a talking part, but this is a feature that reduces the titanic force of his first incarnation in the earlier film. Through uniting Shelley and the Bride through the figure of Lanchester, Whale's film posits a radical view of the literature–film relationship in which the film-maker is the creator and the author, the monster, a creature whose destruction is inevitable. This prologue to the second *Frankenstein* can be seen to look forward as much as backward to the earlier film in which the author is similarly insulted, demoted and destroyed.

The 1931 *Frankenstein* also departs from the novel in its Shakespearean touches. The film begins in a graveyard with a Hamlet-like Frankenstein (played by Colin Clive) lurking in the shadows, accompanied by his sidekick, Fritz, who Horatio-like becomes a soundboard for Frankenstein to explain himself.

Figure 4.4 *Frankenstein* (Universal, James Whale, 1931)

But this Frankenstein is more Macbeth-like in his insatiable desire for power as is implied in the scene in which Elizabeth, Victor Moritz and Dr Waldman try to gain entrance to the Watchtower where Frankenstein is about to give birth to the monster, a 1930s version of Shakespeare's Porter Scene. The insertion of a Shakespearean inflection here, albeit probably accidental, seems surprising within the context of a film that, above all, aims for popular appeal.

Again, following *Dracula*, words are replaced with silence: the increasingly articulate monster of Mary Shelley's tale becomes a mute in Whale's film,[26] suggesting like *Dracula* before it, that horror is at its most terrifying when silent. The film's narrative comes to us not directly from Mary Shelley but through Peggy Webling's 1927 theatrical adaptation adapted by Garrett Ford from an unproduced American version revised by Francis Edward Faragoh. There were also uncredited contributions by Robert Florey and John Russell, further distancing the narrative from that of Mary Shelley. The decision to include the change in the monster made in the theatrical versions from a talking to a silent figure was a significant one, analogous to the decision to transform Dracula's perfect English into a broken or minimalist English, a forgotten aspect of the movies, especially given the newness of sound in the period in which they are produced.[27] An audience, very much alert to the novelty of sound cinema, were presented with a contrast between two types of film: one, reviving recent memories of silent cinema (the monster), the other, almost a parody of the new, heavily theatrical, talkie (represented by Frankenstein, played by Colin Clive whose origins in theatrical acting are more than apparent in his over-the-top performance as the mad scientist). Within a sound film and at a time when actors who were required to speak were imported from the theatre, often to the chagrin of established film

---

[26] Fritz, too, was originally to be mute but was required to speak so as to draw out the character of Frankenstein.

[27] Spadoni, while avoiding comparison to Shelley's novel suggests the monster evokes silent Expressionist cinema calling up memories 'not as it once existed' but 'as it was coming to appear in viewers' memories' (114). He could have argued the same for the overtly histrionic performance of Colin Clive, who conjures up memories not necessarily as theatre existed but as it came to be represented on screen: exaggerated and unnatural.

actors, Karloff's silent monster, even more so that Lugosi's Dracula, implicitly passes judgement on his seeming superiors, upstaging the 'talkie' and overtly theatrical features of the movie.

Like *Dracula* and *Frankenstein*, Paramount's *The Strange Case of Dr Jekyll and Mr Hyde*, released on the last day of 1931, was subjected to heavy censorship and came to film via the theatrical adaptation of the novella. When re-released in 1936, when the full Production Code was enforced, the film lost 8 minutes, largely the sexual content of the scenes with Ivy Pearson (played by Miriam Hopkins). When MGM remade the film ten years later with Spencer Tracy in the lead role, the company bought the rights to the film and recalled all prints of the earlier version, willing it to obscurity for decades. The film, like John Robertson's film of 1920, starring John Barrymore and based on the 1887 popular melodramatic play by Thomas Russell Sullivan, adapts the plot to centre around a love interest. Three days after the first performance of Sullivan's play, the first potential victim of Jack the Ripper was discovered; and the play, and Hyde, in particular, became indelibly linked with Jack the Ripper. Shades of the Ripper are present in the 1931 film, scripted by Samuel Hoffenstein and Percy Heath. As the central character of the novella is split into two, so too are the women in his life: 'bad girl' Ivy Pearson (played by Miriam Hopkins) and fiancée, Muriel Carew (played by Rose Hobart).

In contrast to Tod Browning, the Russian-American director, Rouben Mamoulian was known for his creative use of sound.[28] Subjective photography, using the camera in place of the character, Jekyll, opens the film, so that the viewer is positioned as if they are Jekyll, we see through his eyes, from the first sequence when he appears to us for the first time, two minutes forty seconds into the film, in a mirror. This use of subjective photography is especially effective in the transformation scenes, when we see, with him, our reflection, in the mirror as Hyde. The mirror, so important in the film, is introduced late in the novel when Jekyll recounts his purchase of a mirror in order to observe his transformations. While Hyde begins life

[28] Vieira, 41.

as a humorous child-like character, delighted and visually liberated by his transformation which seems to serve as a valid critique on the restraints of Victorian society (the director described the portrayal of Fredric March as 'the young animal released from the stifling manners and conventions of the Victorian period'),[29] he ends as a horrifying, sexual predator and sadistic murderer. Like him, the audience are drawn in to experience a sense of liberation and titillation followed by degradation and shame as we look with him in the mirror at how far we have descended through the experience of the film.

Described as animalistic or 'Neanderthal' by Greg Mank,[30] Hyde becomes increasingly villainous, with his colour disturbingly darkening, potentially a deeply unpleasant covert reminder for a 1930s audience of why society is so segregated. His associations with Othello cannot be overlooked in his strangulation of the blonde and fair-faced Ivy, both repelled and attracted to Hyde's blackness. One of the film's cuts was Jekyll's passage through a garden path on his way to his engagement party where he hears the sound of a nightingale. The sight of the bird inspires him to quote Keats's *Ode to a Nightingale*,

Thou wast not born for death, immortal Bird!
No hungry generations tread thee down.[31]

The verse is interrupted by the sight of a cat stealthily climbing a tree, an announcement of the imminent death of the bird. Jekyll's face drops and he repeats 'Thou wast not born for death' and for the first time a transformation occurs without the use of the potion, as we see the face of Hyde emerging as he repeats 'Thou wast not born for death'. The recitation of Keats's poem replaces the potion (recalling the poet's imaginative transformation, 'as though of hemlock I had drunk, / Or emptied some dull opiate to the drains') and leads to Hyde's gravitation to Ivy (who he now refers to as his 'little bird, my starling') and to her violent death at his hands. This sequence inverts Keats's poem in which the speaker momentarily transcends death through

---

[29] Quoted in Vieira, 47.
[30] Mank provides a commentary on the film in the 2002 Warner Bros. Entertainment Inc DVD *Dr. Jekyll and Mr. Hyde*: 'Two Feature Films on One Disc'.
[31] *Ode to a Nightingale, Selected Poems & Letters of Keats*, ed. Robert Gittings (London: Heinemann, 1966), ll.51–2.

his identification with the disembodied singer: Jekyll turns into Hyde, from Keats's 'immortal Bird' to instrument of death. The episode underlines the film's 'literariness', perhaps its acknowledgement that it is based on a literary classic, as reflected in the publicity materials, the literary intertextual references and the presence of art, especially the numerous paintings and sculptures scattered throughout the film. Indeed, the use of Stevenson's literary classic was seen as a way of justifying what would otherwise be censored by Head of the Studio Relations Committee, Colonel Jason Joy, who generously felt that 'since it was built upon a literary classic, the Hyde horrors might be permissible'.[32] Placing art within the frames has now been identified as a marker of the adaptation genre,[33] and enables Mamoulian to echo the message of the publicity materials, visually emphasizing that this film is based on art. But, in the film, the artworks can also 'speak' when words are not permitted. Ivy's sexual degradation by Hyde for instance is made apparent through the painting of a naked woman behind her (the sight of which was significantly reduced in the censored version)[34] and the painting and sculptures frequently appear as silent commentators on the action, replacing the words that cannot be spoken on screen. The attack on Ivy by Hyde, who announces himself for the first time to her as Jekyll, is within a set crowded with paintings and sculptures, including a statue of what looks to be the Virgin placed on a shelf below a naked seated woman, reflecting the proximity of Muriel and Ivy, the good and bad women in the film.

Ivy's strangulation by Hyde is inverted and complicated by the statue and paintings behind the 'couple', in particular the copy of the sculpture of Eros and Psyche by Antonia Canova (in what looks like a rape is really a rescue by Eros of Psyche) flanked by two paintings of women, their naked legs echoing Ivy's gartered swinging leg that so attracted Jekyll in his first meeting with her. Ivy's swinging leg, evocative of the pendulum of a clock,

---

[32] Quoted by Mank.

[33] For attempts to identify adaptation as a genre, see Thomas Leitch, 'Adaptation, the Genre', *Adaptation* 1:2 (2008): 106–20, Christine Geraghty, 'Foregrounding the Media: *Atonement* (2007) as an Adaptation', *Adaptation* 2:2 (2009): 91–109, Deborah Cartmell, '*Pride and Prejudice* and the Adaptation Genre', *Journal of Adaptation in Film & Performance* 3:3 (2010): 227–43.

[34] Mank, 44 minutes into the film.

Figure 4.5 *Dr. Jekyll and Mr. Hyde* (Paramount, Rouben Mamoulian, 1931)

is superimposed on Jekyll and Lanyon as they leave her apartment at the beginning of the film, visualizing the strong impression this leg – or Ivy's sexuality – has made on Jekyll at the beginning of the film, indeed it is the beginning of his downfall.

Figure 4.6 *Dr. Jekyll and Mr. Hyde* (Paramount, Rouben Mamoulian, 1931)

The Canova sculpture replaces the actors in the following frame, accompanied by the sounds of Ivy's last breaths.

Figures 4.7 and 4.8 *Dr. Jekyll and Mr. Hyde* (Paramount, Rouben Mamoulian, 1931)

The images disturbingly suggest that Ivy has got what she always wanted: Jekyll. The horrific murder is juxtaposed with an object of beauty, the sculpture depicting the rescue of Psyche by Eros, implicitly deifying the murderer, replacing pain with pleasure. The artwork in the mise en scène serves to underline the artistic ambition of the film and to speak a language that echoes, expands on and complicates that spoken by the actors, who are far from mouthpieces of Robert Louis Stevenson. Indeed the defining image in this film is the mirror, always close at hand, commencing with Jekyll's first appearance on screen, not as himself, but as a reflection of himself. The film revels and triumphs in itself as a 'copy'.

The horror films which appeared in the 1930s were huge commercial successes, somehow appealing to audiences in the thick of the Depression, as the narrator from *Boo* explains: 'With times as tough as they are, we present our formula for the cheapest kind of amusement: nightmares.' Universal took this to heart, becoming identified with the horror genre. Exploiting the perceived appetite for horror in times of economic downturn, an avalanche of horror films appeared within a few years: among them, *Murders in the Rue Morgue* (Universal, 1932), *The Old Dark House* (Universal, 1932), *Freaks* (MGM, 1932), *The Invisible Man* (1933), *Mystery of the Wax Museum* (Warner Brothers, 1933), *The Mummy* (Universal, 1933), *Island of Lost Souls* (Paramount, 1933), *King Kong* (RKO, 1933), *The Black Cat* (Universal, 1934) and *The Raven* (Universal, 1935). In *The Black Cat* Karloff and Lugosi play deadly rivals (as they were, in a sense, at Universal) in a film loosely based on Edgar Allan Poe. In the last film, *The Raven*, Lugosi's character as doctor and

Poe enthusiast ('more than just a hobby') indulges in revenge, disfigurement and torture, with Karloff's character Bateman becoming Dr Vollin's (Lugosi's) 'creature'. Numerous shots, from *Dracula* and *Frankenstein*, in particular, are reconstructed in order to pay homage to the earlier Universal films, suggesting again, the primacy of the film sources over the literary hypotexts. In an article in *Adaptation*, Kyle Dawson Edwards focuses on Vollin's (Lugosi's) climactic statement 'Poe, you are avenged' as a 'key to deciphering Universal Pictures' general approach to film adaptation'[35] in which the literary author is identified as monster, just as was suggested was behind the casting of Elsa Lanchester as both author and monster in Universal's *Bride of Frankenstein*. But, for me, the key is in the motif within the film of the raven's shadow on the wall, like that of the black cat in the earlier film, a powerful meta-textual assertion of the superiority of the shadow (the film) over the literary sources it ostensibly reflects.

To conclude, the 1931 *Frankenstein* and *Dr Jekyll*, consciously or unconsciously, invite comparisons to literary precursors, while all three films pay homage to their origins in silent cinema. The shadows and mirrors so prominent in these three films (perhaps unwittingly or accidentally) reflect their superior status as copies, perhaps unwittingly endorsing the marketing strategies that shamelessly strive for popularity by covering all angles so as to appeal to a mass audience. The victory of the shadows inverts the Platonic idea of the copies as infinitely inferior to the forms they imitate. This is what William Hunter in the first volume of F.R. Leavis's *Scrutiny*, published shortly after these films' release, bemoans as 'the art-form of democracy', cheap mass-produced copies, available and understandable to all.[36]

Reading these films, not as horror, but as gothic adaptations or self-conscious 'copies' of their hypotexts presents them in a different light, as works which are liberated from the 'originals', like Walter Benjamin's assessment of mechanical reproductions, in an essay written five years after these films, an essay which reflects a generation's interest in the threats and

---

[35] Kyle Dawson Edwards, 'Poe, You Are Avenged!': Edgar Allan Poe and Universal Pictures' *The Raven* (1935)', *Adaptation* 4:2 (2011): 117–36, 118.

[36] William Hunter, *Scrutiny*, May 1932, 61–8.

potential of the 'copy'.[37] The sound/silent dichotomy present in all three films works to devalue words over images, a daring strategy at the time of filming, when so many films, such as *King Kong* (1933), which as Stanley Cavell has observed, seem terrified of silence.[38] The sheer act of abandoning words, of those spoken by the monsters, Dracula and Frankenstein, in particular, seems counterintuitive in a period of sound, but one which results in films that have more to say and have endured longer than their more verbose contemporaries. Far from forgetting their literary legacy (as is clear in the marketing strategies adopted in all three cases and in the films' intertextual references to other authors, in particular Shakespeare and Keats), the films take themselves very seriously as adaptations – but adaptations that regard themselves as superior to their 'sources' in their persistent foregrounding of the shadow, mirror, or copy of the 'original'.

---

[37] Walter Benjamin, 'The Work of Art in the Age of Mechanical Reproduction', in *Illuminations* (London: Pimlico, 1999), 211–44.

[38] Stanley Cavell, *The World Viewed* (1971 enlarged edition Cambridge, MA and London: Harvard University Press, 1979), 152. It has to be noted, however, that films were by 1931 no longer so eager to foreground their sound effects as noted by Spadoni, 78.

5

Biopic Adaptations:
Adapting Charles Laughton

The 1930s can be described as the heyday of the biopic, regarded as a subgenre of the historical film, although the many films released within this period do not entirely conform to the genre as we have come to know it today and the name 'biopic' was yet to be imposed on films portraying the life of an individual. The Oxford English Dictionary gives 1947 as the year in which the term first appeared.[1] Historical films have been divided into historical epics, biopics, period musicals and adaptations of classic literature, even though all these genres can be classified as adaptations, that is adaptations of historical events, personages and literary texts.[2] Movies depicting the lives of famous persons are united in their attempts to visually recreate the individuals at the hearts of these films.

These adaptations of the lives of the famous speak very much in the language of their perceived audiences, appealing to a fascination for stardom, both the stars played and the stars playing them. Significantly, the films in this chapter pay little heed to verbal authenticity, an oddity in the early days of sound when you would expect to hear Henry VIII's 'authentic' voice or hear Elizabeth Barrett reading one of her poems (perhaps a reason why this genre, at least anecdotally, has become the most despised amongst historians). Rather, it is the sets and the actors' physical portrayals that dominate. Visually, these biopics 'get inside' their subjects through recreating private places for

---

[1] *OED* cites *Variety*, July 23, 1947, www.oed.com/view/Entry/19243?redirectedFrom=biopic#eid, accessed 15 October 2014.

[2] J.E. Smyth, 'Hollywood as Historian, 1929–1945', in *The Wiley-Blackwell History of the American Film, Volume II: 1929–1945*, ed. Cynthia Lucia, Roy Grundmann and Art Simon (Malden, MA: Blackwell, 2012), 465–7, 474.

the delectation of their audiences, appealing to what seems to be an insatiable appetite, as the fan magazines of the period demonstrate, for what goes on behind the closed doors of Hollywood's famous mansions.[3]

The classical Hollywood biopic is the subject of George F. Custen's *Bio/ Pics: How Hollywood Constructed Public History*, a book which starts at the beginning of the sound period. While not explicitly stated, it is implied, given the starting point of the book, that sound is a pre-requisite for the genre. There are, of course, earlier examples of historical or biographical films, notable examples are George Méliès' *Jeanne D'Arc* (1899) and Abel Gance's 6-hour *Napoleon* (1927). According to Custen, many of the talking biopics encapsulate a tradition of Hollywood mythmaking, focusing on individual agency and aspiration but within a 'mass-tailored contour for fame in which greatness is generic and difference has controllable boundaries'.[4] A snapshot of the major studios' biopics from 1927 to 1938, is adapted here from Custen's study[5]:

MGM (13)
1928
The Viking
1930
Billy the Kid
1932
Rasputin and the Empress
1933
Queen Christina
1934
The Barretts of Wimpole Street
Viva Villa!
You Can't Buy Everything

---

[3]   See Anthony Slide, *Inside the Hollywood Fan Magazine: A History of Star Makers, Fabricators and Gossip Mongers* (Jackson: University Press of Mississippi, 2010).

[4]   George F. Custen, *Bio/Pics: How Hollywood Constructed Public History* (New Brunswick, NJ: Rutgers University Press, 1992), 26.

[5]   Ibid., 242–6.

1936
The Gorgeous Hussy
The Great Ziegfeld
1937
Conquest
Parnell
1938
The Great Waltz
Marie Antoinette

Paramount (5)
1927
Madame Pompadour
1928
Kit Carson
1934
Cleopatra
The Scarlet Empress
1938
The Buccaneer

RKO (6)
1935
Annie Oakley
1936
Daniel Boone
Mary of Scotland
1937
The Toast of New York
Victoria the Great
1938
Queen of Destiny

Twentieth-Century-Fox (10)
1934
Affairs of Cellini
The House of Rothschild
The Mighty Barnum

1935
Cardinal Richelieu
Clive of India
1936
The Country Doctor
The Prisoner of Shark Island
Reunion
1938
Five of a Kind
Suez

United Artists (5)

1930
Du Barry, Woman of Passion
1934
Catherine the Great
Nell Gwyn
1938
The Adventures of Marco Polo

Universal (2)

1935
Diamond Jim
1936
Sutter's Gold

Warner Brothers (11)

1929
Disraeli
The Divine Lady
The Royal Box
1931
Alexander Hamilton
1932
I Am a Fugitive from a Chain Gang
1933
Voltaire

1934
Madame Du Barry
1936
The Story of Louis Pasteur
The White Angel
1937
The Great Garrick
The Life of Emile Zola

Hollywood produced over fifty films in this genre in the sound period, with MGM topping the list, with subjects ranging from those of fugitives, royalty, artists, scientists and politicians. In spite of the number of films produced over this period, there has been no sustained study of these films, movies that together developed many of the features of the late twentieth, early twenty-first-century biopic. While not labelled 'biopics', these film biographies were beginning to take on what has become a recognizable shape.

Rick Altman distinguishes 'genre games': that of the critic and that of the producer. 'The Critic's Game' is itemized by Altman as follows:

1. From industry or critical sources, glean the existence of a genre.
2. Analysing the characteristics of the films most often identified with genre, establish a description of the genre.
3. Scouring filmographies, compile a full listing of films that share enough generic traits to be identified as belonging to a genre.
4. On this basis, begin analysis of the genre.

'The Producer's Game' is somewhat different:

1. From box-office information, identify a successful film.
2. Analyse the film in order to discover what made it successful.
3. Make another film stressing the assumed formula for success.
4. Check box-office information on the new film and reassess the success formula accordingly.
5. Use the revised formula for the basis for another film.
6. Continue the process indefinitely.[6]

---

6 Altman, *Film/Genre* (Bassingstoke: Palgrave, 1999), 38–9.

In his analysis of the biopic, playing 'The Producer's Game', Altman begins with *Disraeli* (Warner Bros, 1929), a film that at the beginning of the sound era was a commercial success and won the leading actor, George Arliss, an Academy Award for his portrayal of Britain's first and only Jewish Prime Minister. Five years after its release, the pressbook attempts to define the film, identifying its unique selling points and describes it as 'a piece of living history'.[7] The biopic, as we know it, has yet to be born but a formula, based on its most popular features, is very much in production as is evident from the marketing of the film.

Dennis Bingham tracks the early 'biopic' of the Studio Era as influenced by Lytton Strachey's myth-making *Eminent Victorians* (1918). For example, the notion of a chosen one is traced to Strachey: 'Destiny and vocation bestow the work of God upon certain people. They suggest powerful belief systems and explain why the biopic, and most literary biography too, is usually not palatable to skeptics'.[8] For Bingham Strachey's novelistic restructuring of the biographical subject by setting them against opposing forces, such as bureaucracies, opposing families or corrupt systems, easily lent itself to the Hollywood biopic. The biopic, a genre so dependent on its star, shamelessly tapped into fan's obsessions with the life of the stars, in particular where they lived and what their houses looked like.

The fan magazines can be seen to participate in a form of what Altman calls 'the Producer's Game', capitalizing on the perceived demands of their readership's insatiable curiosity about famous people's private lives. *Photoplay*, for instance in the early 1930s, is punctuated with glimpses of the homes of the stars. Articles such as 'How They Manage Their Homes: Walk right in – Mr and Mrs Walter Morosco want to show you their new home',[9] '*El Sueno*, "The DREAM" home of the Sills, is a transplanted bit of old Spain',[10] 'COLLEEN Has a House-Warming' '*Some exclusive photographs of the new home of the*

[7] Pressbook, 1934.
[8] Dennis Bingham, *Whose Lives Are They Anyway?: The Biopic as Contemporary Film Genre* (New Brunswick, NJ: Rutgers University Press, 2010), 37.
[9] *Photoplay*, 1929, https://archive.org/stream/photoplay3637movi#page/n73/mode/2up, accessed 6 March 2014.
[10] Ibid., March, 1930, https://archive.org/stream/photoplay3738movi#page/n345/mode/2up, accessed 6 March 2014.

John McCormicks in swanky Bel-Air,[11] 'The Palace of a Laughing King, First Published Views of Harold Lloyd's Great California Estate'[12] and perhaps most enticing of all, 'The Private Life of Greta Garbo, What Goes on Behind the Closed Doors That Hide the Glamorous Garbo from a Prying World'.[13] The article, 'The Robinson's Buy A New House',[14] epitomizes the appeal of these pieces, normally featuring photographs of a façade, an ornate or antique piece of furniture with the star adoringly gazing upon it, a panoramic view of at least one of the downstairs rooms and finally, the star's bedroom, settings we have come to expect in biopic films.

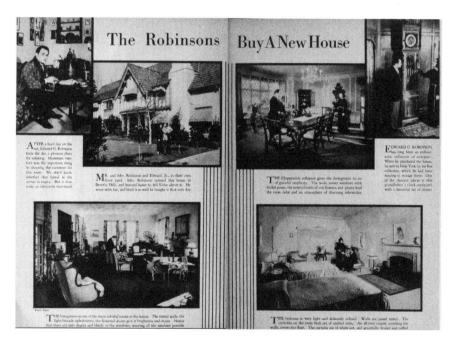

Figure 5.1 *Photoplay*, May, 1934

[11] Ibid., April, 1930, https://archive.org/stream/photoplay3738movi#page/n463/mode/2up, accessed 6 March 2014.

[12] Ibid., May, 1930,https://archive.org/stream/photoplay3738movi#page/n607/mode/2up, accessed 6 March 2014.

[13] Ibid., September, 1930, https://archive.org/stream/photoplay3839movi#page/n335/mode/2up, accessed 6 March 2014.

[14] Ibid., May, 1934, https://archive.org/stream/arphoto46chic#page/n553/mode/2up, accessed 21 March 2014.

These fantastical homes are often combinations of the old and the new, like historical films themselves, contemporary individuals within lavish recreations of famous mansions or styles of the past. The places are described by the journalists with an erotic vigour, addressing their readers directly and intimately with an enticing invitation to follow the stars through the door, up the staircases and right into their bedroom: 'Walk right in'; the stars 'want to show you their home'. The houses of the stars are depicted in a manner reminiscent of Jane Austen's account of Elizabeth's first acquaintance with Pemberley where she is given a more intimate perspective on Darcy. These homes are lavish, sexy, exotic and intimate reflections of the people who inhabit them. The articles aim to lure the reader into sacred places, a technique echoed in the biographical films of the sound period.

The presentation of history as gossip accounts for the perpetual bad reputation of the biopic genre, almost always derided by scholars with vested interests in the subject. As mentioned earlier, the biopic had not been invented until much later as Altman contends: 'Genres begin as reading positions established by studio personnel acting as critics, and expressed through film-making conceived as an act of applied criticism.'[15] The genre – if it exists at all – emerges as both a kneejerk interpretation of a film's popular features, as seen in the *Disraeli* pressbook in its attempt to identify the film's selling points, and as a result of a long-term examination of a film's commercial merits. It is immediately apparent that the biographical film was seen as a profitable product in the sound era. Among the most prominent are *Abraham Lincoln* (1930, starring Walter Huston), *Alexander Hamilton* (1931, starring George Arliss), *The Private Life of Henry VIII* (1933, starring Charles Laughton), *Queen Christina* (1933, starring Greta Garbo), *Voltaire* (1933, starring George Arliss), *The Rise of Catherine the Great* (1934, starring Elisabeth Bergner), *The Barretts of Wimpole Street* (1934, starring Norma Shearer), *Cleopatra* (1934, starring Claudette Colbert) and *Rembrandt* (1936, starring Charles Laughton). In the late 1930s, William Dieterle gained reputation as a director of biographical films with *The Story of Louis Pasteur* (1936) and *The Life of Emile Zola* (1937). The latter, Academy Award winning film, climaxes in a dramatic trial scene, in

---

[15] Ibid., p. 44.

which Zola risks his reputation and everything he has worked for in order to secure the release of the wrongly accused, Alfred Dreyfus. Although mention of Dreyfus's Jewishness is excised from the film, the choice of subject, Zola's oscillation between the desire for a comfortable life and fighting for what he believes in, must have matched the mood of many in the 1937 audience.

The biographical film, or biopic, has since become an obvious route to best actor and actress (most recently, Daniel Day Lewis for *Lincoln*, 2012, Meryl Streep for *The Iron Lady*, 2011 and Colin Firth for *The King's Speech*, 2010) and an opportunity for the studio to capitalize on a star's appeal through the portrayal of a famous personality. Within the early sound period both Arliss (*Disraeli*, 1929) and Charles Laughton (*The Private Life of Henry VIII*, 1933) received best actor awards for their portrayal of historical figures. In praise of *Disraeli*, the 1934 pressbook proclaims 'Every great actor's name is linked in dramatic history with one role', implying that it is the actor who somehow finds a connection with the historical person that drives the film.[16] The remediation of a famous life on film was and continues to be commercially viable, perhaps due to the double-effect of a fascination with famous people and the famous individuals playing them. By reading the biopic as a vehicle to exploit the marketability of a single star, this chapter will look at the 'recycling' of Charles Laughton, identified as the quintessential Englishman, through his role in adaptions of historical figures within a period of five years: *The Private Life of Henry VIII* (1933, directed by Alexander Korda, scripted by Lajos Biró and Arthur Wimperis), *The Barretts of Wimpole Street* (1934, directed by Sidney Franklin, adapted from the Rudolph Besier play by Ernest Vajda, Claudine West and Donald Ogden Stewart) and *Rembrandt* (1936, directed by Alexander Korda with writers Carl Zuckmayer, June Head and Lajos Biró). The latter two films, through the use of Laughton, recycle *Henry VIII*'s successful ingredients: visual authenticity, celebrity status and spatial attentiveness.

The Private Life of Henry VIII, made by London Films, released in 1933, was a commercial success in the United Kingdom and the United States, injecting new hope into the British film industry[17] and watching it today it

[16] *Disraeli*, Pressbook.
[17] Peter Miles and Malcolm Smith, *Cinema, Literature & Society* (Beckenham Kent: Croom Helm, 1987), 168.

is not hard to see how it must have appealed to audiences intrigued by the notorious lives of Hollywood stars, like Henry, in and out of marriage, a subject at fever pitch in Hollywood's gossip columns. *Motion Picture* (January 1934) refers to the film's star as quintessentially British and to Henry as 'the marrying monarch', latching on to two of the major selling points of the film, its combination of an historical British setting with contemporary Hollywood concerns.[18] *Henry VIII* plays straight into the hands of film fans intrigued by the marital mayhem in Hollywood, a subject which unsurprisingly dominated the magazines which offered numerous glimpses of the stars' Henry VIII-like lives, at a time when divorce rates were very low and divorce itself was stigmatized. *Photoplay* not only incessantly reports on Hollywood divorces, with titles like 'How about Mary and Doug?', 'I HAD TO LEAVE JOHN GILBERT' or 'MERRY EX-WIVES of Hollywood',[19] it even attempts to analyse the phenomenon, for instance interviewing 'Dr. Paul Popenoe, Chief of Los Angeles Institute of Family Relations' in order to find the answer to the question 'What's Wrecking Hollywood Marriage?'[20]

The film's oxymoronic title, *The Private Life of Henry VIII*, encapsulates what Gaston Bachelard describes as the 'the dialectics of outside and inside', viewing the king externally and internally, as king and private person.[21] Laughton's real wife, Elsa Lanchester plays Henry's fourth wife (Anne of Cleves), strategically exploiting the audience's interest in the historical figure with a fascination for the actor playing him, allowing us to see the famous living couple in the bedroom together, almost as if we are entering their house, through an article in *Photoplay*. While a British film, Korda's strategy seems to be to appeal to an American and British audience through the blatant use of Hollywood marketing strategies, an obsession with divorce and private lives. The attempt to appeal to a mass audience can be seen in the hit-and-miss

[18] *Motion Picture* (January, 1934), 'You Don't Know Acting Until You Know Laughton', http://archive.org/stream/motionpicture46moti#page/40/mode/2up/search/laughton, accessed 29 October 2014.

[19] *Photoplay*, August, 1930, https://archive.org/stream/photoplay3839movi#page/n191/mode/2up, accessed 30 May 2014, *Photoplay*, April, 1934, https://archive.org/stream/photo46chic#page/n415/mode/2up, accessed 30 May 2014, *Photoplay*, January, 1934, https://archive.org/stream/photo46chic#page/n55/mode/2up, accessed 30 May 2014.

[20] Ibid., October, 1933, http://archive.org/stream/photoplay4445chic#page/n395/mode/2up, accessed 30 May 2014.

[21] Bachelard, *The Poetics of Space* (Boston, MA: Beacon Press, 1994), 211–31.

approach of the pressbook which suggests school tie-ins, and remarking on the film's edifying historical content, while implicitly linking the film to *Dracula*, copying Universal's success, with an image of a vampire-like Henry and the catchline, 'Every woman got it in the neck – eventually'.[22] Exhibitors were urged to display a castle in their lobbies, commission a wrestling show and an eating competition, appealing to those with interests ranging from British history, physical violence and the grotesque.

The film omits Catherine of Aragon (the intertitles following the credits explain 'her story is of no particular interest – she was a respectable woman') and presents the audience to both Anne's and Catherine's executions as if they were watching a film. A conversation between a man and wife, watching the beheading of Anne, is blatantly like a couple watching a movie, with the couple commenting on the event as if it was a fiction on a screen:

Man:	Well, one must admit, she died like a queen.
Woman:	Yes. And that frock, wasn't it too divine?
Man:	Was it? I didn't notice.
Woman:	No, you wouldn't. You wouldn't notice that I haven't had a new gown for a year.
Man:	All right, all right, you shall have one … for *your* execution!

The presentation of the execution as a scene from a movie is no doubt inspired by *The Sign of The Cross* (DeMille, 1932), featuring Laughton as Nero, whose staged spectacles from elephants stomping on chained human victims to Christians being massacred by ravenous lions are within a setting disconcertingly resembling a motion picture house. The spectators, some indifferent, others horrified, provide a meta-commentary on the film audience, watching the same spectacle of violence. Like *The Sign of the Cross*, *Henry VIII* implicitly insults the audience through the association of filmgoers with the voyeuristic thrill seekers attending real violent spectacles, knowingly reflecting on the contemporary audience's devaluation of history as seen in the opening which begins with the external shot of Hampton Court, immediately replaced with the king's chamber, where ladies of the court, like tourists or

---

[22] *The Private Life of Henry VIII*, Pressbook.

devotees of celebrity gossip, greedily gaze at the still warm bed belonging to the king himself. The invasion into the king's privacy (a technique familiar to readers of fan magazines) is both satisfying and disturbing as Korda seems to be both pandering to a public intrigued by the private life of stars while critiquing it at the same time.

While the film itself simultaneously mocks and employs the Hollywoodization of history, the film was marketed as historically authentic, in particular, through the inspiration of Hampton Court which it takes pains to recreate. Laughton personally researched Hampton Court in preparation for the film, insisting designer and brother of the director, Vincent Korda, visit as well. Vincent Korda, indeed, produced what he claimed to be an exact replica of the great hall and declared that the architecture dominated the film.[23] Laughton insisted upon the authenticity of the movie in February, 1934, in an interview in *Film Weekly*: 'most of the dialogue was copied straight from contemporary records of Henry's actual words…. As a matter of fact the only incident in the whole picture for which we can't quote historical chapter and verse is the card-playing scene with Anne of Cleves. And even that is surmisable, I think'.[24] Laughton himself puts his conception of Henry VIII down to the architecture of Hampton Court: ' … I spent a lot of my time walking around the old Tudor Palace at Hampton Court, getting my mind accustomed to the square, squat architecture of the rooms and the cloisters. I think it was from the architecture of the houses and the rooms that I got my idea of Henry'.[25] The account of Hampton Court ('square, squat') applies to Henry himself, reminding us of Vitruvius's conception of architecture reflecting the human form, the man reflected in the building.

Certainly, Charles Laughton's portrayal takes pains to adapt Hans Holbein's portrait at every possible opportunity (Holbein is even a character in the film). But in spite of Laughton's claims of authenticity, the film's script changes Henry into a contemporary figure and cements him as the boorish uncouth, poultry bone hurling but somehow loveable king we know him as today. While visually

---

[23] Greg Walker, *The Private Live of Henry VIII* (London: I.B. Tauris, 2003), 20.

[24] Quoted in Ibid., 34.

[25] *Sunday Express* interview quoted in Simon Callow's, *Charles Laughton: A Difficult Actor* (London: Methuen, 1987), 60.

aspiring to visual historical authenticity, the film's language enables Henry to be reinvented as a modern Hollywood mogul, a buffoon with a sycophantic court artificially hanging on his every word, with lines more suggestive of a Hollywood actor than a Tudor king. Like Shakespeare's *Henry VIII*, Korda manages against all the odds to maintain a level of sympathy for Henry throughout, even in his darkest moments. We are spared his ill treatment of Catherine of Aragon and his involvement in the events leading up to Anne's execution. Jane Seymour, portrayed as selfish and shallow, dies off-screen and once gone is not missed. Henry is made into a victim in the Catherine Howard downfall, transformed by her death from an imposing monarch (who filled the frame in the initial stages of the film) to a very small figure. After Catherine's execution, the mise en scène belittles him: he becomes a shrunken figure silhouetted in the distance and framed by an imposing arch with the tomb of a dead king in the foreground. Henry is looked down upon and dwarfed both by the imposing architecture and by his dead ancestors, now an insignificant figure within the historical canvas.

Altman suggests that *Disraeli*'s success was initially attributed to its 'Britishness' and this film, while explicitly introducing Hollywood features in its dialogue, such as Henry's assessment of Jane Seymour as 'a stupid woman' (he opines to Thomas Culpeper, 'If you want to be happy, marry a stupid woman'), celebrates and critiques Britishness through the figure of Henry, a figure to both admire and ridicule. The juxtaposition of the ornate historical exterior and what goes on behind the scenes is the major selling point of the film – in spite of his pomp and ceremony, Henry comes across as a very ordinary, at times pathetic figure. Made by an immigrant at a time when immigration was seen as a threat to 'Britishness', Korda's film was unsurprisingly attacked by some for its historical inaccuracy and its misrepresentation of Britishness. The Historical Association in 1935 issued a resolution, declaring concern 'at the effect on children and adults of films purporting to represent historical personages which are being shown in picture palaces, and considers that steps should be taken to assist teachers and others to estimate the accuracy of such films'.[26]

---

[26] Quoted by Ibid., 34.

For the Historical Association – and for historians and literature scholars in general – the film was a step too far and it has become an exemplar of the Hollywoodization of history. But Korda's Hollywood treatment of Henry and the consequent gentle debunking of the British was a major part of the strategy to appeal to an American audience; and Laughton replays a version of the self-centred British patriarch in his next biopic, MGM's *The Barretts of Wimpole Street*, directed by Sidney Franklin. The MGM film can be seen to capitalize on *Henry VIII's* presentation of the British and its exposure of the private person through the penetration of the outer walls. The pressbook for this film asks the question: 'What does a poet's room look like?'[27] It claimed that the film constructs the room from the description given by Elizabeth Barrett herself in a letter in which she describes her 'prison' to Robert Browning. The room itself, significantly a bedroom, is the set for much of the film, with the busts of Chaucer and Homer prominently displayed. Indeed, the fetishization of this room within the house foregrounds the theme of writing in the film as a whole and the exposure of the writer's room, like the bedroom in *Henry VIII*, makes the private life a public one.

While *The Private Life of Henry VIII* takes us from the impressive façade of Hampton Court to the bedroom of the king, Sidney Franklin's *The Barretts of Wimpole Street* (adapted in 1934 from the 1930 play by Rudolf Besier and starring Norma Shearer) depicts the bedroom as prison and the film is punctuated by Elizabeth's escapes from the room which become increasingly daring as the film develops: most dramatically her descent out of her room and down the staircase to meet the admiring Browning (played by Fredric March, coming to the role after *Dr. Jekyll and Mr. Hyde*, 1931, *The Sign of the Cross*, 1932, *The Affairs of Celini*, 1934). Her re-emergence in the public space downstairs, however, is thwarted by the arrival of her father, Edward Moulton-Barrett (Laughton). His presence causes a relapse and Elizabeth suffers the indignity of being carried back up the stairs by this patriarchal jailor in the manner of a bride being carried across the threshold and into her bedroom by a husband (perhaps recalling the ending of Tod Browning's *Dracula* in the

[27] Pressbook.

rescue of Mina).[28] Laughton's imposing figure appears throughout the film, at the door of Elizabeth's room, visualizing his role as barrier to the poet's liberation from the deadening claustrophobia of her room, which in the film appears to be the very cause of the poet's illness. On her final escape, she descends the staircase for the last time, brushing against the partially closed dining room door where she hears her father's prayer of thanks for what they are about to receive.

Indeed the stern Christianity of the father is invoked as a tool to imprison his family; he makes Elizabeth's younger sister (played by Maureen O'Sullivan) swear on the bible belonging to her mother that she will never see the man she loves again. Paul Buhle and Dave Wagner include the film in their book, *Radical Hollywood*, observing it is a movie that daringly creates 'a woman's alliance against patriarchy'.[29] But Elizabeth's bold escape from this patriarchal enslavement is covertly also a liberation from the inflexible Christianity that her father advocates. When so many of Hollywood's elite were of Jewish descent, having fled to America as a result of persecution, the critique of the restraints of Christianity must have struck a chord with some audiences. Shearer herself converted to Judaism in 1927 in order to marry the MGM producer, Irving Thalberg. As a result of Nazi rule in 1933 Germany and its policy of Aryanisation, the purging of Jews from the cultural and economic spheres in Germany, many Jewish film-makers fled to America only to see films made by Jews abroad banned in Germany. Thomas Doherty has written about the period of 1933–39 in which the realization of Nazism only slowly emerged in Hollywood; the studios, dependent on Germany for income, maintained an embargo on anti-Nazism and placated their German audiences by virtually erasing 'Hollywood's most prominent ethnic group from the Hollywood screen'.[30] The film needs to be seen within a context in which overt radicalism is impossible, as Paul Buhle and Dave Wagner observe: 'A widespread

---

[28] See Chapter 4 above for a discussion of *Dracula* (Browning, 1931).

[29] Paul Buhl and Dave Wagner, *Radical Hollywood: The Untold Story* (New York: New Press, 2002), 30.

[30] Thomas Doherty, *Hollywood and Hitler 1933–1939* (New York: Columbia University Press, 2013), 45.

suspicion of Jews and Jewish influence – the frequency of asides about the "Franklin D. Rosenfeld" administration, about Jewish promoters ... made it difficult even for monied Jewish conservatives to argue against the tolerance of left-wing ideas held by respectable figures.'[31] But if the Germans cannot be the enemy, the British can.

Laughton's Britishness (and the residue of Henry VIII) sets him apart from Canadian born Shearer and American March and the central thrust of the film is the need to escape, from Barrett and all the British values he seems to represent. Unlike *The Private Life of Henry VIII*, *The Barretts of Wimpole Street* is about escaping the bedroom rather than getting into it. As such, the personal potentially becomes political in a climate of censorship and exclusion. And Laughton's Britishness is implicitly associated with tyranny and an undeserved, deeply flawed sense of superiority, which must have had a particular relevance for a large proportion of the film's audience.

Within this period, Laughton played Nero in *The Sign of the Cross* (1932), Dr Moreau in *Island of Lost Souls* (1932), Horace H. Prin in *White Woman* (1933), Ruggles in *Ruggles of Red Gap* (1934), Inspector Javert in *Les Misérables*, Bligh in *Mutiny on the Bounty* (1935), Rembrandt in *Rembrandt* (1936) and Claudius in *I, Claudius* (1937 – although never completed). While an eclectic range, the thread of biopic parts runs through this period and it is hard to miss Henry VIII's imprint on all of the post-1933 roles. *Rembrandt*, also produced by London Films, recalls the earlier biopic in the many wives (or mistresses) of the painter, Saskia (who dies at the beginning of the movie), Geertje Dirx (played by Gertrude Lawrence) and Hendrickje Stoffels (played by Elsa Lanchester). The theme of failed relationships echoes the numerous accounts of Hollywood divorces, a topic which, as indicated above, litters the pages of fan magazines, such as *Photoplay*, during this period. The film, however, inverts the earlier biopic, with Laughton's Rembrandt an otherworldly character, whose lifestyle belies his artistic greatness (while Laughton's Henry's ordinariness is contrasted to his opulent surroundings). The pressbook capitalizes on

---

[31] Paul Buhl and Dave Wagner, *Radical Hollywood*, 58–9.

Laughton's previous roles inviting us to identify the parts from a 'GALLERY OF GREAT LAUGHTON ROLES'[32] and locates Laughton and Lanchester in a picture quiz with other famous couples in 'KNOW *Your Married Screen Stars?*' The pressbook invites comparisons with *Henry VIII* throughout in banners, such as '*The Private Life of an Artist*' and in articles welcoming the magical reunion of director and actor: 'UNITED FOR THE FIRST TIME SINCE "HENRY VIII"'.[33] Readers are led to believe that the film will be charged with romance: 'Man of genius ... lover of beauty dipping his brush into a woman's secret soul ... feeding the fires of his genius with reckless abandon'.[34] Credits adorning an artist's pallet are accompanied with the ultimately misleading words: 'HE KNEW LOVE AS NO MAN EVER DID! When women moved across the vista of his life ... all kinds and all creeds .... He knew their beauty as no man ever did!'[35] Rembrandt's collection of women is implicitly compared with that of Henry VIII and one image includes Laughton's head encircled by five semi-clad women with a devil in the corner, in an effort to attract those who may be put off by the seemingly highbrow nature of the film as promised in its title. The film is marketed at both intellectuals and pure pleasure seekers, hailed as a crowd pleaser and an artistic 'masterpiece' 'that will have an irresistible appeal to the masses and classes!'[36] In short, it is promoted as a remake of *The Private Life of Henry VIII*.

The film begins and ends with Rembrandt spending money he does not have on art supplies, a need which is depicted as a force beyond his control. Rather than showing the paintings themselves (as Dennis Bingham observes, peculiarly missing from the film),[37] it is Rembrandt's words that captivate his audiences: the film begins with a monologue delivered on the virtues of his wife. But it is his Biblical readings and re-tellings of the Bible to the beggar (who sits for the portrait of Saul), to his father and to the frolicking youths

---

[32] *Rembrandt*, Pressbook, 1937.
[33] Pressbook.
[34] Ibid.
[35] Ibid.
[36] Ibid.
[37] Bingham, *Whose Lives Are They Anyway?*, 45.

at the end of the movie which stand out for leaving their on screen audience spellbound.[38] Laughton's Rembrandt is a poet and a painter and we see the paintings painstakingly recreated in Laughton himself (visually re-enacting Rembrandt's earlier to later self-portraits) as well as in the mise en scène, for instance the cinematic framing of the beggar sitting for Saul (who wipes his eyes with the curtain after being gripped by the painter's story of the king) replicates Rembrandt's actual painting, *Saul and David*.

Figure 5.2 *Rembrandt* (London Film Productions, Alexander Korda, 1936) Compare to Rembrandt, *Saul and David* (Mauritshuis, The Hague, ca. 1655–60)[39]

Set designer Vincent Korda together with George Périnal's lighting create Vermeer-esque interiors.[40] As in *The Private Life of Henry VIII*, architecture plays an important role. The artist begins the film in a seemingly labyrinthine town house then moves to his father's house near Leiden and ends up in a modest abode with Hendrickje (played by Elsa Lanchester), where he is liberated to paint without the contamination of commercial advantage.

---

[38] Charles Higham writes in *Charles Laughton: An Intimate Biography* (New York: Doubleday, 1976) that these readings were later adapted in Laughton's live performances and 'were among his greatest achievements' (70).

[39] A link to the painting can be found at http://www.artbible.info/art/large/378.html, accessed 29 November 2014.

[40] Higham, *Charles Laughton*, 70.

Echoing *The Private Life of Henry VIII* is the bedroom, to which Rembrandt returns after Saskia's death at the beginning of the film, leaving as Henry did before him, to follow her siren-like replacement (Geertje Dirx) into another bedroom in his vast house.

Figure 5.3 *Rembrandt* (London Film Productions, Alexander Korda, 1936)

Figure 5.4 *The Private Life of Henry VIII* (London Film Productions, Alexander Korda, 1933)

Both films begin with a glimpse of the bedroom and call attention to the spectator's voyeuristic delight in looking at the private place of a public person. Architecture, however, functions very differently in these movies: in *The Private Life of Henry VIII* it ultimately serves to dwarf Henry within enormous spaces built to impress whereas in *Rembrandt*, the houses become smaller as the artist becomes larger in relation to his space; a visual metaphor for his increasingly significant place within history. While Henry's diminishment by his house reflects his unworthy place in history, Rembrandt's increased stature within his diminutive country abode intimates his historical importance. An enduring biopic theme emerges in this film; in order to achieve fame, Rembrandt has to almost entirely abandon his social and material ties.

Laughton's next biopic *I Claudius* (directed by Josef von Sternberg and produced by Korda), described by the director as a movie 'to show how a nobody can become a god',[41] was never completed and only survives in parts. From what remains of the abandoned film, it is clear that Laughton's performance is outstanding with his speech to the army and senators likened by the actor Dirk Bogarde to Laurence Olivier's St Crispin's Day speech in *Henry V* (1944).[42] The surviving footage shows Claudius combining the humanity and intelligence of Rembrandt with the imperial presence of Henry VIII.

Graham Greene astutely observed that *Rembrandt*, like *Henry VIII*, failed because 'no amount of money spent on expensive sets, no careful photography, will atone for the lack of a story "line", the continuity and drive of a well-constructed plot'.[43] In this the *Barretts of Wimpole Street* succeeds, even though it implies, contrary to Virginia Woolf's *A Room of One's Own*, published four years earlier, in which a private space for women is seen as essential to liberation, that the poet needs to be rescued and can achieve happiness only at the hands of a man. *Rembrandt*'s failure, however, could also be attributed to Laughton, the quintessential British actor, portraying a man we admire rather

---

[41] Ibid., 113.

[42] Dirk Bogarde, 'The Epic that Never Was, *I Claudius* (1966)', http://www.youtube.com/watch?v=Ll0i6IDrbaA, accessed 15 October 2013.

[43] Review of *Rembrandt*, 1936, reprinted in Graham Greene, *The Pleasure Dome: The Collected Film Criticism 1935–40*, ed. John Russell Taylor (London: Secker & Warburg, 1972), 117–20.

than despise. It is entirely likely that we can credit Laughton's performances in this period as responsible for forging an association of the British male voice with a sinister intent, the voice a safe signifier for the villain, when other accents were too politically sensitive to bring into disrepute. *Mutiny on the Bounty* (1935) is a prime example with a cast that includes Charles Laughton, British villain, Clark Gable and Franchot Tone, American heroes (their accents are retained even though they are playing British parts).

The 'biopic' evolved quickly in this period and the features soon became fixed. The subject, must be made to fit into the sets/houses designed for them and the configuration of space is used to empower or disempower these historical subjects. Significantly, Laughton as Henry VIII is seen in various nooks and crannies, in the state rooms as well as the private rooms, a free agent but one whose ageing is reflected, like that of Rembrandt's, in relation to the narrowing of the space surrounding him. Shearer, as Elizabeth Barrett is trapped in her space with Laughton playing a father who functions to close and barricade doors; her development is reflected in the widening of her spaces as she moves from the excessively restricted domestic to the public sphere, albeit only made possible through the influence of another man.

Returning to Altman's notion of genre as work in progress, or Hollywood's search for a successful formula, we can identify at least three features of these films that stand out and become defining qualities of what has become the identifiable biopic of the twenty-first century.

Visual authenticity

Firstly, each of the films discussed pays particular attention to portraiture, painstakingly recreating 'iconic' portraits of the subject, most notable in *Henry VIII* through the unmistakable similarities of Laughton's Henry to the Holbein portrait, culminating in *Rembrandt*, a film that stands out for recreating the artist's portraits through the framing of the actor as Rembrandt in his many self-portraits. These 'living pictures' or 'tableau vivants' draw attention to the difference between the still and moving image, bringing the subject 'alive' for the viewer.

Figure 5.5 *The Private Life of Henry VIII* (London Film Productions, Alexander Korda, 1933)

Compare to Hans Holbein, the Younger, 1536/7, Walker Art Gallery, Liverpool[44]

Figure 5.6 *Rembrandt* (London Film Productions, Alexander Korda, 1936)

Compare to Rembrandt, 'Self Portrait at the Age of 63' (1669), National Gallery[45]

---

[44] A link to this painting is at: http://www.liverpoolmuseums.org.uk/walker/exhibitions/henry/court.aspx, accessed 29 October 2014.

[45] A link to this painting is at: http://www.nationalgallery.org.uk/paintings/rembrandt-self-portrait-at-the-age-of-63, accessed 29 October 2014.

In *The Barretts of Wimpole Street*, Norma Shearer initially sacrifices glamour for a forced resemblance to Elizabeth Barrett, but one which is softened as the story advances, as her face becomes less hidden by ringlets and her dresses become lighter, less stiff and more revealing.

Figure 5.7 *The Barretts of Wimpole Street* (MGM, Sidney Franklin, 1934)

Compare to Portrait of Elizabeth Barrett Browning by Michele Gordigiani, 1858, National Portrait Gallery[46]

By the close of the film, Elizabeth is transformed, both physically and emotionally: she is translated into the movie star Norma Shearer, stylish, glamorous and self-assured.

The experience of watching is analogous to viewing a painting and, while we as spectators may not be consciously aware of the actual painting being recreated before our eyes, the impression created is analogous to a cinematic visit to an art museum as the films continually remind their audiences that they are based on both real people and on art. But the art is improved by the Hollywood makeover, what was identified in the *Disraeli* pressbook as 'living history' is really the Hollywood version of history, implicitly an 'improvement'

---

[46] A link to this painting is at: http://www.npg.org.uk/collections/search/portrait/mw00856/Elizabeth-Barrett-Browning, accessed 29 October 2014.

on the original. Nonetheless, the visual authenticity and the absence of any attempt at verbal fidelity plays into the long-held notion that film-makers can produce only visual history[47]; there is little attention to the accuracy of the words spoken.

Presence of the star

The second feature is the presence of the star, resulting in the genre becoming as Belén Vidal has identified a 'ubiquitous vehicle for award worthiness' 'particularly when it comes to star making performances'.[48] Famous historical personages were in need of well-known stars to capture their fame for a star-obsessed audience. These cinematic biographies were not a far cry from the manufactured authorized biographies of the stars themselves which as Tino Balio has argued were often based on the narrative roles played by the same star.[49] A fascination for biography, as seen in the rise of gossip columns in fan magazines, was carried over to radio's successful 'Calvacade of America' which showcased stars in famous historical roles, among them Clark Gable, Lionel Barrymore, Tyrone Power and, of course, Charles Laughton.[50]

Spatial attentiveness

The third feature is the architectural sets. These 1930s films depicting famous persons rely on the houses to provide the authenticity that the narratives and dialogue lack and to comment on their subjects' historical value. The development of each historical figure is reflected in the space that they inhabit, through their movements through the house and the size and the splendour of

---

[47] J.E. Smyth, 'Hollywood as Historian, 1929-1945', 477.

[48] 'Introduction: The Biopic and Its Critical Contexts', in *The Biopic in Contemporary Film Culture*, ed. Tom Brown and Belén Vidal (New York: Routledge, 2014), 1–32, 2.

[49] Tino Balio, 'Selling Stars: The Economic Imperative', in *The Classic Hollywood Reader*, ed. Steve Neale (London: Routledge, 2012), 209–26.

[50] Balio, 'Selling Stars', 223. Shearer, married to Irving Thalberg, the film's producer was chosen for the part over Marion Davies, the protégé of William Randolph Hearst who in an act of revenge kept the name of 'Norma Shearer' from appearing in any of his newspapers.

the rooms they inhabit. The places provide both a sense of historical credibility and privileged access to the interiority of the subjects.

Oddly for movies made in the new era of sound, none of these films make any serious attempt to be true to the individual's words but focus instead on how historical personages look and where they live, shamelessly in order to attract an audience obsessed by stars and their private lives. By multiplying the appeal of the star subject with a star performance, the movies let us, as greedy spectators or nosey neighbours, get inside their lives through entering the homes they live in. The interiority of the principle subject is explored through the insides of the houses, exploiting an audience's fascination with stars' private lives while implicitly comparing their legendary status to the historical personages they portray. In this respect, *The Private Life of Henry VIII*, the first British film to attract a major American audience and the first British film to receive an Oscar,[51] provided a template for many biopics to come. It adapts Hollywood marketing strategies with a very British subject, reformulating history so that the film creates *the* Henry VIII for generations to come, poking fun at itself and the British to the apparent delight of an American audience.

---

[51] *Picture Play Magazine*, December, 1933, http://archive.org/stream/picturepl39stre#page/n863/mode/2up/search/laughton, accessed 15 April 2014.

6

Adaptations for Children:
From Pre-Code to Post-Code Hollywood

Adapting well-loved children's narratives to the talkie brought with it new challenges and concerns regarding morality and literacy. Stories, meant to be read, and instil a love of reading in children, were seen to be under threat in the era of the new talkie, when a book was no longer needed in order to supply the missing words. Unsurprisingly, a striking feature in the press materials is the prominence of the book with the message that the book will be opened, not closed, by the presence of the film. Adaptations, directed at children, were also relentlessly marketed on their wholesomeness: these films were sold on the basis that they were entertaining, educational and above all, clean. Adaptations, directed at children in the 1930s, are read here in relation to growing concerns about the power of films to corrupt and the consequent threat of shrinking audiences and diminishing box-office returns. Adaptations were, to a degree, reinvented, as guarantors of safe, wholesome and educational entertainment, in an attempt to rescue the movies' sinking reputation as a promoter of idle and lascivious behaviour.

The imposition of the Production Code during this period encouraged films that were appropriate for children, but as Richard Maltby argues, the Code 'was a consequence of commercialism and of the particular understanding of the audience and its desires that the industry's commercialism promoted'.[1] In other words, the Code was not just the brainchild of a few influential moralists and educationalists, but a response to consumer demand. The

---

[1] Richard Maltby, 'The Production Code and the Hays Office', in *Grand Design: Hollywood as a Modern Business Enterprise, 1930–1939*, ed. Tino Balio (Berkeley: University of California Press, 1995), 37–72, 72.

Catholic National Legion of Decency was formed in 1933, in response to 'morally objectionable' films, such as *Baby Face* and *I'm No Angel*, as a means to eradicate 'the pest hole that infects the entire country with its obscene and lascivious motion pictures'.[2] Essentially, arising from the new possibilities of the talkies, the regulation of film content moved from a mode of recommendation to one of enforcement, described by Robert Sklar as 'The Golden Age of Turbulence' (1930–33) and 'The Golden Age of Order' (1934–).[3] In response to rising concerns about the moral value of cinema and the damaging effects on audiences, particularly on the young, three 'General Principles' were devised in 1934:

> 1. No picture shall be produced which will lower the moral standards of those who see it. Hence the sympathy of the audience shall never be thrown to the side of crime, wrong-doing, evil or sin.
> 2. Correct standards of life, subject only to the requirements of drama and entertainment, shall be presented.
> 3. Law, natural or human, shall not be ridiculed, nor shall sympathy be created for its violation.[4]

The detrimental effects of motion pictures on children, like mobile phones today, was an unknown quantity and there was much concern surrounding children's morality and education, in particular literacy, arising from the new talkies. A five-year research programme by the Motion Pictures Research council (1929–33), *Pictures and Youth* was summarized in Henry James Forman's best-selling *Our Movie-Made Children* (1934).[5] In the introduction to the volume, W.W. Charters, Chairman of the Committee on Educational Research of the Payne Fund, recommends that 'whole-hearted and sincere cooperation of the producers with parents and public is essential to discover how to use motion pictures to the best advantage of children'.[6] Even the fan magazines sided with these anxieties. An article in *Picture Play Magazine*

[2]   Quoted in Thomas Doherty, *Pre-Code Hollywood: Sex, Immorality, and Insurrection in American Cinema 1930–34* (New York: Columbia University Press, 1999), 320.
[3]   Quoted in Maltby, 'The Production Code and the Hays Office', 38–9.
[4]   'A Code to Govern the Making of Talking, Synchronized and Silent Motion Pictures', MPPDA, 1930, quoted in Maltby, 'The Production Code and the Hays Office', 48.
[5]   Henry James Forman, *Our Movie-Made Children* (New York: Macmillan, 1934).
[6]   https://archive.org/details/moviemadechildre00formrich, accessed 20 May 2014.

(October 1933) admits that *Movie Made Children* touched a sore spot and concludes that 'it may cause parents to check up on films that children are allowed to see, thereby cutting down box-office receipts'.[7] In response to anxieties regarding Hollywood films' potentially corrupting influence on young audiences, during the period, 1934–35, study guides sponsored by the National Council of Teachers of English were attached to prestige productions to promote the educational value of these movies. In 1934, Carl Milliken, Secretary of the Motion Pictures Producers and Distributers of America, made the announcement that 'the list of authors whose works will appear on the screen during the 1934–35 season is headed by Dante, Shakespeare, Dickens, Poe, Tolstoy and Dumas', emphasizing that these films were in the making prior to 'the healthy, nation-wide discussion of clean pictures'.[8] Likewise, Will Hays promised cinema audiences that the 1934–35 season would witness 'a very large increase in the number of films being made from the great classics of literature and the stage and from books that have already won a place in the hearts of millions of readers'.[9] It seems that the National Legion of Decency were, in part, responsible for the rise of 'classic adaptations' in this period, perpetuating the view that adaptations of 'quality' books are good for you (failing to note the violent landscapes and contentious content of writers such as Dante, Poe and Tolstoy).

In light of concerns over cinema's effects on the young in the 1930s and the general consensus that adaptations of classic novels are 'safe', this chapter will consider the talkie children's adaptation, in particular *The Three Little Pigs* (directed by Burt Gillett, scripted by Boris V. Morkovin, 1933), *Little Women* (directed by George Cukor with a screenplay by Sarah Y. Mason and Victor Heerman, 1933), *Alice in Wonderland* (directed by Norman Z. McLeod with a screenplay by Joseph L. Mankiewicz and William Cameron Menzies, 1933), Disney's *The Country Cousin* (directed by Wilfred Jackson and written by Dick Rickard, 1936), Disney's *Thru the Mirror* (directed by David Hand and written by William Cottrell, Joe Grant and Bob Kuwahara, 1936), *Wee Willie Winkie* (directed by John Ford with a screenplay by Ernest Pascal and

---

7 http://archive.org/stream/picturepl39stre#page/n711/mode/2up, accessed 27 June 2014.
8 Quoted in Maltby, 'The Production Code and the Hays Office', 63.
9 Quoted in Thomas Doherty, *Pre-Code Hollywood*, 333.

Julien Josephson, 1937) *Heidi* (directed by Alan Dwan with a screenplay by Walter Ferris and Julien Josephson, 1937) and Disney's *Snow White and the Seven Dwarfs* (directed by William Cottrell, David Hand, Wilfred Jackson, Larry Morey, Perce Pearce and Ben Sharpsteen and written by Ted Sears, Richard Creedon, Otto Englander, Dick Rickard, Earl Hurd, Merrill De Maris, Dorothy Ann Blank and Webb Smith, 1937), the first sound adaptations of much loved stories.

Martin Rubin sees 1933 as a turning point in Hollywood content. Prior to the creation of the Production Code Administration of 1934 which regulated films' content to placate women's groups, religious organizations and educationalists, 'The film industry was placed on the defensive as never before'.[10] Disney's *Ugly Duckling* (1931) is a good example of pre-Code animation. Oblivious to any moral objections, in a new twist to a well-known tale, Ugly Duckling's birth (in which he emerges as markedly different from his siblings and parents) results in the father abandoning his family in the belief that his partner has indulged in an 'extra-marital' relationship. *Babes in the Wood* (1932), an adaptation of *Hansel and Gretel* as recorded by the Brothers Grimm, shows the brother and sister beguiled by a witch into entering the Gingerbread Cottage where they encounter children turned into tortured, emaciated animals, cruelly caged and chained by the witch. The children manage to reverse the spells and capture the witch in her own cauldron. She is able to free herself from the cauldron but in pursuit of the children, she is gradually and painfully transformed into stone. It would be impossible to make these films that depict adultery and the abuse of children a few years later. Disney's animations became more cautious in their choice of content while defensive of the value of entertainment. Rubin describes how Disney's *Three Little Pigs* (1933), which was 'embraced by the public as a Depression-razing allegory', shows how entertainment coexists with a belief in the moral value of hard work.[11] Practical Pig, while working all day, unlike his layabout brothers, keeps the wolf from the door but also

---

[10] Martin. Rubin, 'Movies and the New Deal in Entertainment', in *American Cinema of the 1930s: Themes and Variations*, ed. Ina Rae Hark (New Brunswick, NJ: Rutgers University Press, 2007), 92–116, 95.

[11] Ibid., 108.

enjoys his music in his spare time: managing a healthy work–play balance. Practical Pig is able to save (and ostensibly reform) his brothers and send the lean, dishevelled and dirty wolf, a symbol of the Depression itself, howling into the distance. But, as Rubin notes, the Pigs' lives are not destined to be all singing and dancing, as the portraits of Father (a string of sausages and ham hock, on Practical Pig's wall) augurs that the ultimate sacrifice, for the greater good of the economy, is just around the corner. Although Walt Disney denied any political significance, the film was widely regarded as an allegorical reading of the Depression and interpreted in the left-wing *New Theatre & Film* as an extension of President Roosevelt's appeal to the populace to 'stick together'.[12]

The blockbuster of 1933, *Alice in Wonderland*, directed by Norman McLeod, was a surprising failure as *Variety* predicted on 26 December 1933: 'A series of scattered, unrelated incidents definitely won't do to hold interest for an hour and a quarter'.[13] Indeed it was regarded as 'one of the worst flops of the cinema' by Rob Wagner, finding nothing positive to say about the film.[14] While a box-office flop, due to the costumes, that in an effort to recreate John Tenniel's illustrations render the stars unrecognizable, the pressbook for Paramount's *Alice in Wonderland*, released in December, 1933, boasts the selling power of its stars and the educational benefits of the movie. Lewis Carroll's books were popular property for film in the early sound era, with Walt Disney thinking about a feature-length movie, before *Alice* was released in 1931 by the low-budget Commonwealth Pictures Corporation and then by Paramount in 1933. Among the cast of the Paramount film are Gary Cooper, W.C. Fields, Cary Grant, Edna May Oliver and Charlotte Henry playing the role of Alice (and like all actresses playing Alice after her, she remained relatively unknown). The pressbook is awash with ideas as to how to promote the film's educational value, stressing the movie's closeness to the book. We are told that 'Half the charm and selling power of "Alice in

---

[12] William Kozlenko, 'The Animated Cartoon and Walt Disney', in *New Theatre and Film: 134–37*, ed. Herbert Kline (San Diego, CA: Harcourt Brace, 1985), 284–94, 285.
[13] *Variety* 26 December 1933.
[14] *Rob Wagner's Script* 10 (250) December 23, 1933, 11–12, reprinted in Anthony Slide, ed. *Selected Film Criticism: 1931–1940* (London: Scarecrow Press, 1982), 5–6.

Wonderland" lies in the theme: See these delightful characters step out of the book and come to life!' The pressbook suggests that exhibitors Hire a young girl, dress her in an Alice costume, and place her in the book'. At peak hours, 'Alice' pushes the door open, hands circulars to patrons and then steps back into the book closing the door behind her.[15] The pressbook advertises a study guide with forthcoming school competitions and reiterates the film's fidelity to the book. Indeed, it is described as 'an exact reproduction of the two famous fantasies "Alice's Adventures in Wonderland" and "Through the Looking Glass"'.[16]

Alice's selling power is its innocence. One article in the pressbook, ' "ALICE" WILL END Wise-Cracking Era in America' announces how the film will be wholesome entertainment: 'Motion picture critics who have, over a span of years, watched the influence of the films on national customs manners and life, today are wondering if Paramount's filmization of the beloved classic, "Alice in Wonderland" will bring back to public favour the sweet simplicity of the young girl of that era.'[17] The marketing is unequivocally appealing to audiences' concerns regarding the morality and educational value of cinema. On the whole, it is a very dull film, and wastes its stars behind the costumes with the live action film seeming to emulate an animated feature. Its combination of live action with animation, however, is daring, and the stand out sequence is the animated inset of the Walrus and the Carpenter in which the worldly Walrus with his Carpenter sidekick dupes the baby oysters into leaving their home to follow in a great adventure, an unwitting parallel to the promoters of the picture's promise to its target audiences of pleasure beyond belief: 'Wholly unlike anything done before', 'an artistic masterpiece'.[18] Introduced by Tweedledee and Tweedledum, through a screen inserted in a tree, we see the cartoon as if we are watching a film within a film, the seemingly innocent duo narrating a tale of adult deception. While the animated sequence is itself 'a mini masterpiece', its disturbing content, with children becoming fatal victims of the adults' greedy pleasures, as in the novel, undermines the spirit of adventure

---

[15] Pressbook, 8.
[16] Ibid., 40.
[17] *Alice*, Pressbook, 40.
[18] Pressbook, 40.

and innocence that the narrative seems to celebrate. The reviewer in *Variety* is similarly not fooled by the appeal to children: ' "Alice" is really a distinctly grown-up book. Juvenile patronage probably won't be the choice of the kids themselves, but possibly under grown-up duress'.[19] The Betty Boop cartoon, *Alice In Blunderland*, released a year later more successfully re-presents the story with a not-so-innocent Alice who when falling down the rabbit hole needs to keep her tiny dress from flying up, seemingly acknowledging a more adult audience.

Where Paramount's *Alice* failed, RKO's *Little Women* (released in November, 1933) triumphed. Martin Rubin points out, the film 'vied with Mae West's second release of the year, *I'm No Angel*, for the title of the year's biggest fourth-quarter hit'.[20] As Thomas Doherty argues, the film did much to confirm the profitability of rectitude.[21] *I'm No Angel* and *Little Women* occupy opposite ends of the spectrum: vamp playing West's box-office decline and controversial content versus the model of a reformed cinema and the reign of 'literary-credentialed prestige pictures as Hollywood's most reliable big earners for the rest of the decade'.[22] Will Hays informed B.B. Kahane (RKO's studio head) that *Little Women* 'may open a new type of source material'.[23] The president of RKO Distribution attributed the film's success to its wholesome content: 'the public is hungry for something clean and wholesome – particularly fathers and mothers who have been worried about the movie entertainment that their children have been seeing'.[24] The pressbook covertly addresses audiences' scepticism regarding the moral and educational benefits of film adaptation in its presentation of a poster designed for schools, insisting that schools *will* display it (presumably as a response to the refusal of schools in the past to display 'educational' film publicity). Educationalists are reassured that the 'photoplay is mentioned only incidentally in the text', revealingly acknowledging an awareness of prejudice against movies within educational establishments. But while there is significantly only little mention

---

[19] *Variety* 26 December 1933.
[20] Rubin, 'Movies and the New Deal in Entertainment', 113.
[21] Doherty, *Pre-Code Hollywood*, 333.
[22] Rubin, 'Movies and the New Deal in Entertainment', 113.
[23] Quoted in Maltby, 'The Production Code and the Hays Office', 63.
[24] Ibid., 63.

of the film in the text of the poster, the author of this article in the pressbook adds, 'the illustrations are all from the photoplay'.[25] The 'bookishness' of the film is shamelessly exploited in the suggestion for a 'TRAFFIC-STOPPING WINDOW EYEFUL', a display featuring a giant book with stills from the film, suggesting that a 'pretty girl, perhaps resembling Jo or another of the four sisters, dressed in the style of the Sixties, can be employed to turn the pages slowly'.[26] In hindsight, the pregnancy of Joan Bennett (who played Amy), if widely leaked, could have resulted in the opposite sort of publicity that the movie sought, as epitomized in an advertisement in *Picture Play Magazine*: 'WELCOME, thrice welcome, to the wholesome and reassuring trend in pictures and applause for those who bring to the screen a quartet of heroines who are known in every language.... There isn't a shady lady among them'.[27] Compare this to an advert in the same magazine for Mae West's *I'm No Angel*: 'Yes', says MAE WEST, 'When I'm good, I'm very very good but when I'm bad, I'm better... it's all about a girl who lost her reputation but never missed it. Come up and see it some time'.[28] *Little Women* is regarded as the first film of the decade to take a literary work and adapt it into both artistic and commercial success.[29] RKO's choice of Louisa May Alcott's novel was an astute one as the story directly addresses the reformation of children in hard times, a topic close to the hearts of those concerned about the evil effects of the movies.

The film (which won an Oscar for Sarah Y. Mason and Victor Heerman for best screenplay) juxtaposes the harshness of the war with domestic comforts, rewriting the novel so that Jo becomes the author of the story; one, which through the auspices of her soon-to-be husband, like the battle between pre- and post-Code film, is not sensational, melodramatic or fantastic, but homely and morally edifying. The girls' hardships, in particular Meg's occupation as nursery maid and Jo's as companion, however, seem to be forgotten after the

---

[25] *Little Women*, Pressbook, 1933.

[26] Ibid.

[27] *Picture Play Magazine*, October, 1933, http://archive.org/stream/picturepl39stre#page/n697/mode/2up, accessed 27 June 2014.

[28] Ibid., November, 1933, http://archive.org/stream/picturepl39stre#page/n747/mode/2up, accessed 27 June 2014.

[29] Tino Balio, ed. 'Production Trends', in *Grand Design: Hollywood as a Modern Business Enterprise 1930–1939* (Berkley: University of California Press, 1993), 179–312, 187.

first six minutes of the film. After their first entry into society in which Jo wears a patched dress and the sisters have to share a pair of gloves, there is little evidence of poverty. Implicitly, with the return of the father is a return of the family's fortunes and Jo is able to write for pleasure rather than for money, offering audiences during the Depression hope for an end to hard times.

Jo's Christmas play, performed at the beginning of the film, is reminiscent of an earlier period of melodramatic cinema, with Jo playing a potential rapist to an audience which includes a very disapproving Marmee whose role, like that of the film-makers themselves, is to tone down this dangerous exuberance, transforming Jo, played by Katherine Hepburn, from awkward and daring show-off at the beginning of the film to compliant domestic goddess by the end, from writer of sensational fiction to a writer of homely girls' stories, a narrative which would chime with those concerned about the dangerous effects of Hollywood film on young viewers. The audience sees an improvement in Jo (perhaps contrary to Alcott's narrative)[30] and a corresponding improvement in film, from the wooden old-fashioned and unconvincing acting in Jo's sensational melodrama to the comfortable, secure and homely mood established at the film's close. The prominence of Hepburn's name (at least five times the size of Louisa May Alcott's) and the assertion 'Twenty million have read the book … Fifty million will love the picture'[31] in a *Photoplay* advertisement boasts the superior influence of the film over the book, an ambition at the heart of Disney adaptations.

Disney adaptations in the latter half of the 1930s, similarly, can be seen to echo concerns about film's influence on children, as outlined in *Our Movie-Made Children*. Disney's *Silly Symphonies* offers young viewers a first taste of nursery stories with titles such as *The Ugly Duckling* (1931), *Father Noah's Ark* (1933), *The Pied Piper* (1933), *Who Killed Cock Robin* (1935) and *The Three Blind Mouseketeers* (1936). The *Mickey Mouse* series, all with Mickey as the central character, feature adaptations, such as *Gulliver Mickey* (1934) and *Mickey's Man Friday* (1935). *Silly Symphonies Who Killed Cock Robin* stands

---

[30] For a different reading of the novel, see, Deborah Cartmell and Judy Simons, 'Screening Authorship: *Little Women* on Screen 1933-1994', in *Nineteenth-Century American Fiction on Screen*, ed. R. Barton Palmer (Cambridge: Cambridge University Press, 2007), 77–93.

[31] October, 1933, http://archive.org/stream/photoplay4445chic#page/n503/mode/2up, accessed 26 June 2014.

out in presenting caricatures of Bing Crosby, Mae West and Harpo Marx, culminating in a bird trial scene in which a range of film genres – gangster, musical, romance and slapstick – come together. In the end it is discovered that Cock Robin (the Bing Crosby character) is not dead, merely stunned by Cupid's arrow, leaving him to pursue a romance with sexy Jenny Wren, the Mae West caricature. The adaptation draws more on Hollywood film, in particular star performances, than it does on the nursery rhyme of its title, presumably aimed at an audience of children who would be more familiar with the movies than with the poem. This is taken a stage further in 1938 in *Mother Goose Goes Hollywood*, in which nursery rhyme characters are modelled on stars, among them Katherine Hepburn (Little Bo Peep), W.C. Fields (Humpty Dumpty) and Stan Laurel and Oliver Hardy (Simple Simon and the Pie Man). In See Saw Margery Daw, Greta Garbo and Edward G. Robinson are on a see saw; Garbo complains 'I want so much to be alone', whereupon Robinson responds by getting off the see saw, leaving the precious star an undignified fall. In this adaptation, the stars' 'personalities' take over the characters that they play, just as Disney films usurp their sources, leaving the urtexts all but forgotten.

Anxiety about the contents of cartoons, emanating perhaps from the daring content found at the beginning of the 1930s, was articulated in a 1939 article in *Look* magazine: 'We cannot forget that while the cartoon today is excellent entertainment for young and old, it is primarily the motion picture fare of children. Hence, we always must keep their best interest at heart by making our product proper for their impressionable minds'.[32] It seems that Disney's cartoons are indeed 'motion picture fare', as is evident in the content of cartoons of the latter half of the 1930s.

Filmed in Technicolor, *The Country Cousin* and *Thru the Mirror* are Disney cartoon adaptations features, described by Susan Ohmer as typical of films of 1936 that 'lift us out of material existence into another realm'.[33] However, I suggest, while they offer audiences luxurious images of material pleasures, these features sing the praises of restraint and normality. *The Country Cousin*

---

[32] Quoted in Eric Smoodin, *Animating Culture: Hollywood Cartoons from the Sound Era* (New Brunswick, NJ: Rutgers University Press, 1993), 15.

[33] Susan Ohmer, '1936: Movies and the Possibility of Transcendence', *American Cinema of the 1930s*, 162–81, 81.

(1936) portrays Country Mouse's disillusionment with his slick cousin's stolen lifestyle and the horrors of a Fritz Lang's *Metropolis*-like city life, possibly appealing to a small town American audience, shocked at the excesses of Hollywood. In *Thru the Mirror* (1936), Mickey Mouse falls asleep with an open copy of *Alice Through the Looking Glass* on his bed when a second self emerges from the snoring figure to pass through a mirror, evocative of a movie screen, into a room of animated objects. The sequences replicate in cartoon animation numerous popular films of the period, among them *Top Hat* (1935), Busby Berkeley's choreography in the overhead shot of dancing cards, *The Private Life of Henry VIII* (1933) in the rotund, disagreeable and jealous King of Hearts, Errol Flynn's swashbuckling hero and Tarzan with Mickey swinging on a telephone cord through a jungle of furniture. *Thru the Mirror* concludes with a relieved Mickey back in his bed, safe from a perilous Hollywood-styled world that almost consumed him. The film 'has its cake and eats it too': it draws on many of the features of pre-Code Hollywood while rejecting them in preference for safer and more wholesome domestic comforts.

A change in production trends contributed to the elevation of Shirley Temple, signed by Fox in 1933, to a top box-office star. Temple more than filled the gap for wholesome entertainment, so welcome in post-Code Hollywood.[34] The adaptation *Wee Willie Winkie*, starring Temple, is perhaps most famous for Graham Greene's review (which brought a libel case against him) in which he challenged Temple's wholesome status. In the review, Greene writes that Temple's stardom is 'clever but it cannot last. Her admirers – middle aged men and clergymen – respond to her dubious coquetry, to the sight of her well-shaped and desirable little body, packed with enormous vitality, only because the safety curtain of story and dialogue drops between their intelligence and their desire.'[35] Greene implicitly challenged the studio's adherence to the Production Code and questioned their motives to provide wholesome, morally uplifting films. Temple's team took legal action against the writer. Greene lost and Fox (and Temple) won the battle.

---

[34] Maltby, 'The Production Code and the Hays Office', 64.
[35] Graham Greene, *Night and Day*, October 29, 1937, http://thecharnelhouse.org/2014/02/25/graham-greenes-infamous-review-of-wee-willie-winkie-1937-starring-shirley-temple/, accessed 27 May 2014.

Wee Willie Winkie is based on Rudyard Kipling's short story about a six-year old Colonel's son growing up in India, nicknamed 'Wee Willie Winkie' after the nursery rhyme. The boy rides his pony after a young woman who is defying her fiancée by riding into dangerous territory. When Wee Willie Winkie catches up with her, she has hurt her ankle and is unable to move. The pair become surrounded by malevolent men eager to capture them. However, forward thinking Wee Willie Winkie sends his pony back to his father's regiment as a signal that he is in danger and the regiment respond quickly and come to his rescue. The father expresses his pride in his son for saving the young woman and Wee Willie Winkie, in Kipling's concluding words, entered 'into his manhood' and asks that he be from this day forward addressed by his real name, Percival William Williams.

Beyond the title, the film bears little resemblance to the short story it is based on although it is very much promoted as an adaptation: 'A PICTURE WORTHY OF THE AUTHOR WHOSE HEROIC PEN CAPTURED THE SPELL OF INDIA'.[36] In the film, directed by John Ford, set during the British Raj in 1897, Percival becomes Priscilla and through her trusting nature, befriends the leader of the rebelling Afghan tribe, Khoda Khan (played by Cesar Romero). Through her innocence and charm, she manages to stop the bloodshed between her grandfather's regiment (located in a British colonial outpost near to the Afghan border) and the rebels. While almost unwatchable today, the adaptation challenges Kipling's rigid gender division where women are described as belonging to the men, with Priscilla continually questioning why she is not allowed to be a soldier, like Mott, a drummer boy only a few years her senior. The American, Priscilla and her mother are the voices of common sense, morally triumphing over the British and the rebels, both groups ridiculed for their unquestioning regimental behaviour and prejudices. Greene is right that the film improves on the short story but he would have done better to locate the unwholesomeness of the film in the racial stereotypes it portrays rather than in what he worryingly perceives as the sexualization of its child star.

Unlike the Kipling adaptation, *Heidi*, Temple's next adaptation, did not require radical rewriting. Johanna Spyri's *Heidi*, the story of the young girl

[36] *Wee Willie Winkie*, Pressbook, 1937.

deserted by her aunt and abandoned in the Swiss Alps in the primitive home of her embittered grandfather who she reforms into a doting guardian seems tailor-made for Temple. *Heidi*'s pressbook agrees and unites the novel's character with the movie star: 'IN THE BELOVED STORY MILLIONS WANTED HER TO MAKE' with Temple featured on bookmarks with Johanna Spyri's novel surrounded by letters from fans, all entreating Temple to play Heidi.[37] In the film, Heidi is downtrodden by unscrupulous women: a loveless and opportunistic aunt and the evil governess who attempts to sell Heidi to an even worse Gypsy woman. In contrast, all the men in the film are positive influences, even surrogate mothers, in particular, her grandfather (Jean Hersholt) and the butler (Arthur Treacher) who befriends her in the luxurious home in which she is sold as a companion. Heidi's final choice of the simple life with her grandfather over wealth and social elevation provides a Depression-weary audience with the moral that family life is more important than riches. The film announces itself throughout as an adaptation, 'bringing a book to life', from the opening credits in which the cast are presented through the turning of the pages of the novel to the grandfather's reading of a story in which Heidi is transported to a song and dance number, 'In Our Little Wooden Shoes'.

Snow White and the Seven Dwarfs, the first mainstream animated feature, like the short Disney features discussed earlier, can be read as covertly addressing the concerns of its post-Code audience. It is tempting to see this movie as a response to pre- and post-code Hollywood through the juxtaposition of Snow White and her evil stepmother, a figure Woody Allen's Alvie in *Annie Hall* claims to have preferred, a leaning that he feels explains later neurotic tendencies.[38] So too, the animators of the Disney film had a preference for drawing the Queen over Snow White, as, in her erotic appeal, her all absorbing vanity and Lady Macbeth-like ambition, she was far more interesting than the younger character.[39] On one hand, we have the

---

[37] *Heidi*, Pressbook.

[38] 'You know, even as a kid, I always went for the wrong women. I think that's my problem. When my mother took me to see Snow White, everyone fell in love with Snow White. I immediately fell for the Wicked Queen' *Annie Hall*, Rollins-Joffe Productions, Woody Allen, 1977.

[39] Jack Zipes, *The Enchanted Screen* (New York: Routledge, 2011), 115.

adorable, chirpy Snow White, Shirley Temple-like good girl, who in spite of a dreadful life remains steadfastly optimistic. On the other hand, we have the undoubtedly beautiful Mae West-style evil Queen, who is determined to reap revenge on the little girl who is stealing the show. The figure in the Mirror, like a Hollywood mogul, goads the Queen on to re-establishing her reputation at centre stage, with shades of a pre-Code comeback. As Jack Zipes observes, the Queen never sees her reflection, she sees only the male face in the mirror and significantly it is his voice that dictates to her what constitutes beauty.[40]

Elizabeth Bell equates the evil Queen with femme fatales, such as Greta Garbo and Marlene Dietrich, linking her to later figures such as Maleficent and Ursula, from *Sleeping Beauty* (1959) and *The Little Mermaid* (1989). These evil Disney female figures, stemming from the evil Queen, participate in what she sees as reconstructions of 'feminine excess', the 'layers of rapacious animal imagery [which] align [their] powers with predatory nature'.[41] Both Zipes and Bell read the film in terms of its construction of female identities, but they also read it ahistorically. While I would not go so far as suggesting that the film is a critique of the patriarchal construction of female beauty, it does seem to speak to a contemporary concern with what is deemed most acceptable for post-Code audience consumption. But whether or not we are meant to believe the Mirror (or the film studios that declare their new preference for wholesome values over the risqué), it is Snow White who is identified as the most beautiful, and the modelling of the good girl (with the exception of the hair) recalls Shirley Temple's rather stocky form and chubby face, even though the princess was inspired by the actress, Janet Gaynor. Temple was used to indirectly endorse the film: she posed with two of the dwarfs at the film's premiere and was chosen to present Walt Disney an Honorary Academy Award for the film in 1939. Making cartoons into 'real' stars, as we have seen in *Mother Goose Goes Hollywood*, allows Disney to make the animations seem real. The film invites comparison between animation and

40 Jack Zipes, *The Enchanted Screen*, 122.
41 Elizabeth Bell, 'Somatexts at the Disney Shop', in *From Mouse to Mermaid: The Politics of Film, Gender and Culture*, ed. Elizabeth Bell, Lynda Haas and Laura Sells (Bloomington: Indiana University Press,1995), 107–124, 117.

live action in order to elevate the status of the former, ultimately suggesting that the film takes over and surpasses its literary 'sources'.

The film's narrative structure, especially in its departures from the Brothers Grimm version (*Sneewitchen*), owes something to the typical Temple film, the charming orphan whose innocent demeanour changes lives and minds. Like Temple, Snow White is able to convert even the harshest of men to her cause, from the Huntsman to Grumpy; her prayer in the dwarfs' house, 'Please let Grumpy like me' echoes that of Temple's Wee Willie Winkie who similarly prays to God to let her gruff grandfather like her too. The transformation of Grumpy is the most moving moment of the film, with the once cynical Grumpy uncontrollably convulsing in grief over Snow White's inert body. The sequence depicting the grieving dwarfs is described by John Canemaker as 'the baptism of a new powerful kind of animation' capable of bringing tears to the eyes of the audience.[42] The believability of the cartoon characters dominates the effusive reviews of the film. Typical of these is James Shelley Hamilton's expressions of amazement on first seeing the film: 'It is astonishing how these pictures create a life in a world of their own, totally unreal in fact but absorbingly real to the entranced imagination.'[43] The film proves that animation can be emotionally gripping and that the audience can be involved in the relationships that the film establishes. But the dwarfs' relationship with Snow White is slightly questionable. From a twenty-first-century perspective, Snow White (arguably unlike Temple) is explicitly and disturbingly sexualized by the response she receives from the kisses she gives the dwarfs (in particular, Dopey, who tries to kiss Snow White on the lips and undaunted by her refusals, keeps coming back for more).

In spite of offering an arguably sanitized version of the fairy tale (for instance, Snow White does not make the Queen dance in red hot shoes at her wedding), of all the children's adaptations discussed here, this is 'the fairest of them all'. In the manner of future mainstream Disney adaptations, this film usurps the fairy tale in the minds of its audiences by creatively adapting the story of the Brothers Grimm, perhaps most memorably in giving the dwarfs names and

---

[42] *Snow White*, 2001 DVD commentary.
[43] James Shelley Hamilton in *National Board of Review Magazine* 13 (1) (January 1938): 10–11, reprinted in Anthony Slide, ed. *Selected Film Criticism*, 237–8.

characters, whilst using familiar cinematic experiences to tell the tale. Most striking is the German Expressionist forest in which Snow White finds herself trapped, a sequence that visually resembles Hermia being engulfed by the forest in the 1935 *Midsummer Night's Dream* directed by Max Reinhardt and William Dieterle. The Queen as wicked witch is possibly modelled on the scary 'The Vengeance' from Jack Conway's 1936 *Tale of Two Cities* (and voiced by the same actress, Lucille La Verne). The Queen's descent down the winding staircase recalls Tod Browning's *Dracula* and her underground laboratory can be likened to that of Frankenstein in James Whale's film. Her transformation from beautiful Queen to ugly witch is reminiscent of Rouben Mamoulian's *Dr. Jekyll and Mr. Hyde*. Voices in the film were chosen with extreme care, with Disney commenting on the difficulty he had in finding a voice that was suitable for *Snow White*,[44] with the voice chosen (that of Adriana Caselotti) very much in line with those associated with the musical films of the 1930s. Disney's ambition was to compete with mainstream Hollywood productions and the film seamlessly adapts popular film features, including pre-Code movies, into an animated feature that succeeds both artistically and commercially.[45] The pressbook, unlike the other pressbooks for films discussed in this chapter, shows a noticeable restraint in its suggestions for marketing the movie. Rather than proposing gimmicks to promote the movie, the pressbook calls attention to the Disney's artistry. On the re-release, ten years after the first showing, the pressbook focuses on the film's legacy and its paratexts (party snappers, porcelain figures, jigsaws), positioning it as one of the most loved movies of all times, still on *Variety*'s list of top grossers.[46] The film made profits for RKO of around $8 million and broke the US box-office record.[47]

Jack Zipes has noted that the film retains the patriarchal structure of the Brothers Grimm version, with an emphasis on 'cleanliness, control and organized industry'[48] and much of the film's running time is perhaps not

---

[44] Disney speaking on the *Snow White* DVD commentary.

[45] Ibid.

[46] *Snow White and the Seven Dwarfs*, Pressbook, 1948.

[47] Figures from Douglas Gomery, *The Hollywood Studio System: A History* (London: BFI, 2005), 153.

[48] Jack Zipes, 'Breaking the Disney Spell', in *From Mouse to Mermaid: The Politics of Film, Gender and Culture*, ed. Elizabeth Bell, Lynda Haas and Laura Sells (Bloomington: Indiana University Press,1996), 21–42, 40.

coincidentally devoted to cleaning: Snow White (whose name could be that of a brand of detergent) is first seen in rags scrubbing steps and famously, she cleans the dwarfs' cabin with the help of the woodland animals she befriends, in order to impress the inhabitants that she is worth keeping. Snow White's motherly insistence that the dwarfs wash before sitting down to eat provides numerous comic opportunities, with the dwarfs' stunts possibly echoing the physical comedy, or 'monkey business', of the Marx Brothers; but the emphasis on cleanliness throughout the film also could allude to Disney's commercially astute sanitization of the fairy tale and his embracement of post-Code values in the presentation of clean, wholesome stories. As Eleanor Byrne and Martin McQuillan observe, the dwarf's washing song becomes 'Disney's mantra for the next half-century': 'You may be cold and wet when you're done / But ya gotta admit it's good clean fun'.[49] 'Good clean fun' surely brings to mind 'post-Code' values to an audience in 1937. Although it did not entirely escape criticisms for its presentation of violence (in the United Kingdom, the film suffered some cuts),[50] it seems to have established Disney's reputation as morally uplifting and quality entertainment, as Eric Smoodin observes: 'one year after the triumph of the feature-length *Snow White*, no popular source … questioned the quality, either aesthetic or moral, of Disney animation'.[51]

The promised inclusivity of these movies (entertainment for everyone) and their celebration of innocence together with the narrative of rebirth or baptism (from Heidi's grandfather's to Grumpy's conversion) announce a new kind of film, and a new kind of industry, one that seeks to rediscover a lost innocence. Rather than embracing a new modernity, these films look backwards, resurrecting stories deemed to be both edifying and safe, recovering a sense of past innocence. Many of the mainstream children's adaptations of this period are, like Dickens adaptations, in one manner or another, associated with Christmas, the holiday period that brings families together. *Little Women* begins at Christmas. *Alice in Wonderland* released in America in December 1933, clearly was targeted at audiences during

---

[49] Byrne and McQuillan, *Deconstructing Disney* (London: Pluto, 1999), 62.
[50] Richard Schickel, *The Disney Version: The Life, Times, Art and Commerce of Walt Disney* (1968; rev. Worcester: Pavilion, 1986), comments on some of the complaints from protesting parents that Disney received about the film's violent content, 220.
[51] Smoodin, *Animating Culture: Hollywood Cartoons from the Sound Era*, 14.

Christmas and the pressbook suggests that stores have Alice windows such as 'An "Alice In Wonderland" Christmas! This is the decision of the nation's leading department stores this year'.[52] Heidi's grandfather rescues her on Christmas day and the film offers spectacular Christmas displays, including a magnificent Christmas tree, presents and carol singing. *Snow White and the Seven Dwarfs*, released on 21 December 1937, is similarly, targeted at audiences at Christmas, promising wholesome family entertainment: an inexpensive, guaranteed inoffensive, heart warming present for the entire family.

These adaptations are shaped by concerns regarding the potential evil influence of cinema, seemingly willingly embracing post-Code values. The persistently reassuring promotions of the films as 'safe' and 'innocent', aimed at audiences concerned about the effect of the movies on children, contribute to the stigma attached to film adaptation, one that has never quite gone away. Adaptations, in this period, were often made as antidotes to films presenting crime, violence and sex, and by extension defined themselves through their publicity as morally uplifting, educational and safe. The publicity surrounding the films that unashamedly and unrealistically promised audiences 'exact' and 'definitive' replications of classic novels, in the end, gave adaptations a bad name. For book lovers, the adaptations were dilutions of literary texts and for film lovers, pale versions of what went before in the pre-Code era of innovation and risk. These promotional materials unwittingly perpetuate a perception that adaptations are 'safe' and therefore fundamentally conservative and backwards looking, planting what Robert Stam has identified as 'the roots of a prejudice', 'the intuitive sense of adaptation's inferiority'.[53]

---

[52] *Alice*, Pressbook.
[53] Stam, 'The Theory and Practice of Adaptation', 1–52, 4.

7

Conclusions: Radical Adaptations

While technological advances obviously improved the quality of sound in literary adaptations over the first decade of the sound film, the use of sound, or more precisely the spoken word, could be seen to inflict serious harm on the reputation of adaptations. Adaptations, which are predominantly 'wordy', were perceived as backward looking or fundamentally conservative in both style and content, perhaps in response to the overly zealous and transparently erroneous promotions of these films as carbon copies or even improvements on the stories upon which they are based. The promotional writers' lavish praise turned into the reviewers' patronizing criticism: adaptations were pale copies, slaves to the words of the author, theatrically derivative and historically inauthentic Hollywood simplifications. Adaptations became associated with a certain type of film that is regressive, safe and acknowledged as inferior to the stories that they are 'based' upon. The promotional literature's stress on adaptation's educational value and the valorization of the words of the authors essentially backfired and served to belittle the movies in the eyes of their critics (but not always of their fans), as diversionary and unhelpful guides and pale copies of the books that provide the plot lines of their scripts.

Certain authors thrived in this period, others (Shakespeare most prominently) failed to adapt to the screen in the eyes of both the fans and critics. Some authors, such as Jane Austen, surprisingly did not make an appearance until 1940. Other obvious candidates are also absent. There was one film of *Jane Eyre* in 1934 (Monogram, directed by Christy Cabanne with Colin Clive, carrying shades of Frankenstein as Mr Rochester) and it was not until 1939 that *Wuthering Heights* was released. The 1934 *Jane Eyre* sums up everything that we come to dislike about adaptation; the narrative is almost unrecognizably condensed into just over one hour,

Jane (played by Virginia Bruce) is transformed into a peroxide blonde starlet, an accomplished pianist and highly talented singer (allowing for a musical interlude to show off the film's sound quality), the set is static and stagey and the audience is reminded that the film is an adaptation through the transitions in time that are predictably marked by the shaky turning of the pages of *Jane Eyre*, the novel. As has been noted throughout, the fetishization of the words of the author is a consistent feature of adaptations of classic texts in this period.

In the case of Shakespeare adaptations, the obsession with the reproduction of Shakespeare's words resulted in word-counting exercises and the tendency to judge a film based on the number and pronunciation of words, with the inevitable conclusion that the movies were audacious and wrong-headed attempts to do justice to Shakespeare's dramas. Much of the criticism of the films was criticism of the films as if they were books or plays, leaving the movies with no chance of critically succeeding. Audiences too, it seems, were not interested in films that were overly 'bookish'. Critics such as Harley Granville-Barker were entrenched in the view that cinema was a solely visual medium, the less said, the better: 'Of the cinema's second-best foot – so to call it – the mechanical reproduction of speech, there is little that need yet be said. The delicate colouring and fine gradations demanded by the speaking of poetry are still beyond its technique (in that filmed "Romeo and Juliet" a surprising proportion of the inhabitants of Verona seemed indeed to be afflicted with cleft palates). But bring it to perfection, it will still hardly oust the picture side of the cinema from pride of place'.[1]

Dickens adaptations fared much better, possibly because these narratives appealed to those suffering through the Depression, with uplifting stories about survival in hard times, and the narratives converted more easily into scripts that did not have the same reverential regard for the words of the author. Indeed, silence plays an important part in these film adaptations offering audiences an addition rather than an omission to Dickens's stories. These movies were able to 'say something' new, with less reverence for the figure of the author, by adding silence to Dickens's stories.

---

[1] *The Listener* XVII, 425, 3 March 1937, 387–9.

Gothic narratives were cinematically adapted in a manner that seems to disregard, or call into question, the author's authority. In *The Bride of Frankenstein*, the author, Mary Shelley is implicitly turned into a monster through the casting of Elsa Lanchester, who plays both author and creature. The film's destruction of the author is covertly conveyed through this strategic double casting. These films thrived and were regarded as progressive, perhaps, because they were not defined as adaptations in the way that films based on the work of Shakespeare or Dickens were. It is obvious that the more canonical or revered the author, the more regressive or backward looking the film was deemed, demonstrating a point made much later by Stanley Kubrick, 'If it had been written by a lesser author' then it follows 'it might have been a better film'.[2] In this period, Dickens was still regarded as a popular writer and Shelley, Stevenson and Stoker were not subject to the same amount of critical scrutiny that they are today, perhaps one of the reasons why the Gothic (or Horror) films thrived. As the pressbook for Rouben Mamoulian's *Dr. Jekyll and Mr. Hyde* recommends, the films should put the horror genre first, the story (and, by extension, the author) second.[3]

The biopics, discussed in this book, pay little heed to faithfulness to their subjects' words but rather strive for visual veracity and cashed into their audience's fixation with film stars. *The Private Life of Henry VIII* explicitly and shamelessly 'Hollywoodised' history through the parallels drawn between Henry's reign and Hollywood practices, successfully attracting an American as well as British audience. Charles Laughton's portrayal as Henry – as greedy, tyrannical and over-privileged – fed into his later roles and contributed to the demonization of the middle-aged British male. It is without doubt that Laughton made a major contribution, in the sound period, to the association of the British male accent (a novelty on the sound screen) with moral depravity and hypocrisy, the British being an easy target compared to other accents, in particular, German.

The adaptations that are discussed in this book, which are aimed at children (or based on children's stories), promised their audiences old-fashioned

---

[2] Stanley Kubrick, interview for *Der Spiegel*, on the subject of his adaptation of Nabokov's *Lolita*, quoted in Thomas Leitch, *Adaptations and Its Discontents: From 'Gone with the Wind' to 'The Passion of the Christ'* (Baltimore, MD: Johns Hopkins University Press, 2007), 242–3.

[3] *Dr. Jekyll and Mr. Hyde*, Pressbook, 1931; see Chapter 4, note 13.

values and positioned themselves in opposition to pre-Code films that were alleged to encourage moral delinquency. These adaptations were marketed as embracing the ethos of the Code, a marketing strategy that doomed the movies to a long-standing reputation of being slavishly conservative. The hostility to 'uplift' inoffensive entertainment that can be happily consumed by all, as expressed by Q.D. Leavis,[4] was shared by the literary establishment of critics and writers who did more than their share in denigrating film adaptation as an affront to the novel. But it is worth remembering that those who initially opposed the talkies, such as Aldous Huxley and Graham Greene, ended up changing their minds and working in the industry.[5] However, the view of 'serious' writers on Hollywood adaptations, as epitomized by Theodore Dreiser, prevailed throughout this period and beyond: 'It is not so much a belittling as a debauching process, which works harm to the mind of the entire world. For the debauching of any good piece of literature is – well, what? Criminal? Ignorant? Or both? I leave it to the reader.'[6] Dreiser was, arguably, more concerned about the transformation of his own work, but this dominant view that film reduces rather than creates something new has dominated attitudes to film adaptations, particularly to adaptations of 'classic' texts. It is worth considering how within a period of increasing censorship, adaptations of seemingly safe and much loved works of literature might offer a way out, a platform for saying something new.

In this period, we can see how far film adaptation evolved by comparing two adaptations of *Anna Karenina*, 1927 and 1935, both starring Greta Garbo, a story which as Andrew Britton has observes fits into Garbo's casting as tragically sexually transgressive.[7] The modern dress silent film, directed by Edmund Goulding and starring Garbo and John Gilbert (after an aborted attempt at an adaptation directed by Dimitri Buchowetzki and starring Garbo) changed its name from *Heat* to *Love*, allegedly in order to promote

---

[4] Leavis, *Fiction and the Reading Public*, 192.

[5] For an account of writers' opposition to cinema and adaptations of their works, see Cartmell and Whelehan, *Screen Adaptation: Impure Cinema* (Basingstoke: Palgrave, 2010), 41–56.

[6] Theodore Dreiser, 'The Hollywood Experience', from *Liberty*, June 11, 1932, reprinted in *Authors on Film*, ed. Harry M. Geduld (Bloomington: Indiana University Press, 1922), 206–22, 211.

[7] Andrew Britton, 'Stars and Genres', *Stardom: Industry of Desire*, ed. Christine Gledhill (London: Routledge, 1991), 198–206, 199.

the movie as 'Garbo and Gilbert in *Love*', alluding to the couple's alleged off-screen romance. The film was made with two endings: one in which Anna commits suicide by leaping in front of a train, and another in which after years apart and the death of Anna's husband, the lovers are reunited. The film is marketed as an adaptation ('it is a gorgeous piece of entertainment that has with utter fidelity kept the spirit of the novel')[8] and an irresistible tale of passion (the 'vivid picturization has resulted in the one production that no man or woman in the whole world can resist').[9] However, in spite of promises of steamy passion, the review in *Variety* calls attention to the film's restraint: 'if the censors think they're going to have a picnic through being the only ones permitted to see things, it's going to be an uneventful private showing'.[10] The scenes, especially the kisses, between Garbo and her son, played by Phillipe de Lacy, are worryingly the most passionate of all and John Gilbert's Vronsky is right to look alarmed at his competition for Anna's affections. Tellingly, when in exile in Italy, Anna sees a boy resembling her own and tries to kiss him, the child runs from her in horror, as if he is about to be ravaged. The restraint the *Variety* reviewer noted is key to Garbo's performance as her face reflects little emotion through the majority of the film, with the exception of the scene at the horse race. Rather than focusing on the race, the spectators' gaze falls on Anna's reactions to it and her loss of control while witnessing Vronsky's near victory followed by his near fatal fall. Her un-Garbo-like inability to contain her emotions subjects her to the disapproving gaze of the spectators, a display that is not repeated in the next adaptation of Tolstoy's novel.

Garbo's return to the role in 1935 is directed by Clarence Brown, reputed to be the star's favourite director, with co-star Fredric March. The intertextual marketing strategy for this film could not be further from that of the earlier film; instead of misleadingly promising audiences unlimited steamy passion, the film is advertised as wholesome fun in the manner of Cukor's *David Copperfield*. Young David himself, Freddie Bartholomew, probably the closest

---

[8] Pressbook, 1927, 2.

[9] Ibid., 5.

[10] *Variety*, December 7, 1927. *Variety's Film Reviews 1926–1920*. Vol. 3, ed. R.R. Bowker (New York: Reed, 1983).

thing to a male version of Shirley Temple and who plays Anna's devoted son in a cringe-making performance in which his innocence is far too extreme to believe, links the movie to *David Copperfield* in the film's trailer: 'I hope and believe you will like it just as much as you did *David Copperfield*.'

The film was made allegedly against the better judgement of producer David O. Selznick and lead male actor Fredric March. Selznick writes of the film that the 'trend to the classics on the screen made a new production of *Anna Karenina* almost inevitable' but also the timing of the production was a serious setback, as Selznick explains, the Legion of Decency's objections to unwholesome content were at their most intense.[11] The use of Freddie Bartholomew ('"DAVID COPPERFIELD" HIMSELF!') to advertise the picture and the seal of approval from the Daughters of the American Revolution and Joseph L. Breen, prominent in the pressbook,[12] reflect MGM's desire to market the film as 'innocent' entertainment, a significant challenge given the content of the novel. The pressbook downplays the tragic and controversial nature of the story, selling it almost as a romantic comedy: 'THE NEW GARBO! AS SHE HAS NEVER APPEARED BEFORE. Smiling…. Happy…. Carefree…'.[13] It is hard to imagine anything further from the truth. In 1927, *Love* was deceptively marketed as so passionate 'that no man or woman in the whole world can resist'[14]; in 1935, *Anna Karenina*, in what seems nothing other than a diversionary tactic, is misleadingly sold for its innocence and lightheartedness.

From Selznick's correspondence with Garbo, it appears that it was only Garbo who was enthusiastic about the project. The film, itself, however, makes few announcements that it, like *Copperfield*, is an adaptation. Instead of pages turning or a book opening, the credits at the start of the film, as in its predecessor, *Love*, only mention that it is '*From the novel* by Count Leo Tolstoy'. This pared-down version of Tolstoy's story, scripted by Clemence Dane and Salka Viertel, is marketed more as an adaptation (or remake) of

---

[11] Quoted from William Lavin, ed., *A Guide to the Study of the Screen Version of Tolstoy's Anna Karenina* (Newark, NJ: Educational and Recreational Guides, Inc., 1935). Rudy Behlmer, ed., *Memo from David O. Selznick*, ed. Rudy Behlmer (New York: Modern Library, 2000), 85–7.

[12] Pressbook, 1935.

[13] Ibid.

[14] Ibid., 1927.

Garbo's 'restrained' earlier film, with March made to resemble *Love*'s co-star and former Garbo romantic interest, John Gilbert, with his short hair style and pencil moustache. Although March is made to physically resemble Gilbert, his Vronsky is morally inferior to Gilbert's character and he is reduced to a foil upon which to reflect the greatness of Garbo's Anna. Garbo appears eight minutes into the film, dramatically emerging from a train with her face initially clouded by steam. Once in focus, the camera shares the gaze with Count Vronsky (March), who is immediately smitten. Anna's serenity and dignity is in stark contrast to the world Vronsky inhabits, shown in advance of Anna's first appearance on screen, where he partakes in an extravagant banquet, followed by a marathon drinking competition (which he wins) rounded off in a seedy tavern where he drinks with Anna's brother Stiva and jokingly converses on the subject of marital infidelity. Anna's first appearance signifies that she is clearly better than her contemporaries, superior to the men, in particular, just as Garbo is physically positioned in the film and in the film's publicity as superior to the other actors. A 1935 poster of the film devotes a third of its space to the face of Garbo, who is placidly looking into the distance, with sketches from the film across the bottom. The names of 'Garbo', 'FREDRIC March' and 'FREDDIE Bartholomew' are presented in decreasing font sizes.

The accents on offer are a strange mixture: it is hard to understand how Anna (with Swedish accent) is sister of Stiva (played by Reginald Owen who has a British accent). Fredric March's Vronsky is unmistakeably American and Basil Rathbone, who plays Anna's husband Karenin, is the most British of all (described by the *Variety* reviewer as speaking 'Oxfordese English')[15] and the nastiest of the characters in the film, in keeping with the trend emerging in this period to demonize the British middle-aged male. Garbo's accent singles her out as exotic and unique and isolates her from the other figures in the film.

The film, made just after the rigorous enforcement of the Production Code, as Selznick vividly recalls, compared to its contemporary adaptations, is surprisingly daring in its subject matter. While bowdlerized by the Breen

---

[15] September 4, 1935, *Variety's Film Reviews 1934–37*, ed. R.R. Bowker (New York: Reed, 1983), np.

office into a very pale version of Tolstoy's narrative, it does not, as Thomas Doherty suggests of the post-Code adaptation, entirely erase the 'dark undertones' and 'flatten out' the narrative's ambiguities.[16] In spite of MGM's protestations otherwise, the film not only defiantly represents infidelity but also seems to defend it as a necessary evil in a world of double standards (where men can be unfaithful but women cannot). Anna's betrayal of her husband, given his callous and cold behaviour towards her, is an understandable one and his treatment of her, once she has 'fallen', blackens him even more in the audience's perception.

The scene in the Opera House brings home what is at stake for an adaptation of a tale of infidelity for an ultra sensitive post-Code audience. For the contemporary audience, it is not a far remove from a cinema in the mid-1930s, in which a major section of the audience would refuse to acknowledge Anna and Vronsky as a couple, some of whom would refuse to accept Anna even if she had managed to obtain a divorce. Lea Jacobs reads this sequence as paying lip service to the Code, through a woman dismissing her companion's admiration of the couple with they 'aren't even a couple': in other words, their illicit relationship has no status in society and the film audience should wake up to that fact as well.[17] However, Anna's defiant visit to the Opera House, against Vronsky's objections, turns her, like Garbo herself in real life, into an object of the gaze. The unpleasant aristocratic gossips call into question her right to be seen in public and the camera moves from their prying and censorious comments and disapproving looks to the object of the gaze, the imperious Garbo herself who, as in the beginning of the film, is seen as rising above the society that passes judgement upon her. This juxtaposition of the star with the censors invites comparison with the effects of the Production Code on the film's freedom of expression and its forced subjugation to a system that is blatantly unfair as Selznick laments in his notes to the film: 'Our first blow was a flat refusal by the Hays office to permit the entire section of the story dealing with Anna's illegitimate child. This decision was so heartrending, especially as it meant the elimination of the marvellous

---

[16] Doherty, *Pre-Code Hollywood*, 335.

[17] Lea Jacobs, *The Wages of Sin: Censorship and the Fallen Woman Film, 1928–1942* (Berkley: University of California Press, 1997), 123.

bedside scenes between Anna, her husband and her lover, that we were sorely tempted to abandon the whole project – but what remained of the personal story of Anna seemed so far superior to such inventions of writers of today as could be considered possibilities for Miss Garbo, that we went on with the job.'[18] Although the film omits much of the novel's content (especially Levin's story and Anna's pregnancy), *Anna Karenina* manages, against the odds, to portray a fallen woman who is above all, sympathetic. What remains of Tolstoy's narrative in the film (as Selznick implies more full of possibilities for Garbo than what was allowed by '[screen]writers of today') enables a stretching of the rules of post-Code Hollywood, challenging the enforcement and morality of current film censorship while questioning the 'safeness' of adaptations of classic fiction.

It could be similarly argued that *Becky Sharp*, starring Miriam Hopkins (adapted from Langdon Mitchell's 1899 stage adaptation of Thackeray's *Vanity Fair*), like *Anna Karenina*, adapts the now disgraced fallen woman film in the guise of adaptation. There's very little of Thackeray's novel left here and viewers are more likely to recall Hopkins in earlier roles, in particular as the fallen and victimized Ivy Pearson in *Jekyll and Hyde* and the fallen woman in *The Story of Temple Drake* (1933, directed by Stephen Roberts, an adaptation of William Faulkner's 1931 novel, *Sanctuary*, scripted by Oliver H.P. Garrett and Maurine Dallas Watkins), described by Thomas Doherty as 'a model of pre-Code Morality' in which a question mark is left over whether or not Temple (Hopkins) enjoys 'her degradation'.[19] Flirtatious and frivolous socialite, Temple, is dragged into a world of the desperately impoverished, with those living on the edges of society, victims of the Depression, including a resignedly forlorn woman (played by Florence Eldridge) who puts her unwashed baby in a wood box to protect it from rats. After a horrific ordeal, Temple kills her rapist, and admits to the crime in court, with the closing line of the film spoken by the honest man she initially rejected: 'Be proud of her … I am'. Significantly, the film does not specifically identify Faulkner's harrowing and highly controversial novel, *Sanctuary*, in its credits (it is listed as 'From a

---

[18] Quoted in Behlmer, *Memo from David Selznick*, 86–7.
[19] Doherty, *Pre-Code Hollywood*, 117.

novel by William Faulkner') and the 'adaptation' is a very much diluted and transformed version of Faulkner's story (for instance Temple is raped with a corncob by her impotent attacker in the book, while the film just leaves us literally in the dark). The film still had the effect of shocking audiences, for the all too realistic portrayal of the dehumanizing effects of the Depression and for presenting a woman of 'loose morals' who is raped. Significantly she is redeemed in the film whereas in the novel the rapist becomes almost sympathetic and Temple is corrupted after her ordeal; dependent on gin and sex, she gives false testimony, reaching a sanctuary at the end of the novel that the narrator implies is not altogether deserved. Daringly, *The Story of Temple Drake* empowers Temple, and rather than the shallow exiled figure of Faulkner's novel who is last seen 'in the embrace of the season of rain and death',[20] the film intimates that Temple is not Faulkner's victim of her own desire, but that there may be a future for her, that she may be released from the stigma of the fallen woman through her brave and truthful testimony. The film was removed from circulation in mid-1934.

Directed by Rouben Mamoulian and released in 1935, *Becky Sharp* (screenplay by Francis Edward Faragoh) dazzled the *New York Times* reviewer through its innovative use of colour and it is remembered as the first feature length Technicolor film.[21] Graham Greene, likewise, could only comment on the film's use of colour, giving 'so much delight to the eye that it would be ungrateful to complain of the climax in Bath, the indecisive acting of Miss Miriam Hopkins as Becky'.[22] Moral guardians too might have been blinded by the colour, as the film, like the earlier fallen women or bad girl films, is thoroughly anti-authoritarian in its representation of marriage and adultery. Hopkins portrays Becky as an actress par excellence (who can produce tears to fit any occasion) in a society that is characterized by hypocrisy. Society's objections, in particular the sanctimonious and sneering women's reaction to Becky's sexual flaunting and defiantly rebellious behaviour (like

[20] William Faulkner, *Sanctuary* (Harmondsworth: Penguin, 1980), 253.

[21] Andre Sennwald, 'Becky Sharp', *The New York Times* 14/6/1935, http://www.nytimes.com/movie/re view?res=9C00E1D61139E33ABC4C52DFB066838E629EDE, accessed 21 August 2014.

[22] *The Spectator*, July 19, 1935, Graham Greene, *The Pleasure Dome: The Collected Film Criticism 1935– 40*, ed. John Russell Taylor (London: Secker & Warburg, 1972), 9.

the disapproving women in *Anna Karenina*), echo complaints about the riskier sort of film, by organizations like the General Federation of Women's Clubs or Committee of the Daughters of the American Revolution: 'Pay no attention.... You're too fine to notice such vulgarity' and 'Why did you bring me here?.... This is a wicked and immoral atmosphere'. In *Becky Sharp*, the fallen woman is not the victim, but gets the last laugh. Becky begins as she ends, throwing a book at those who disapprove of her, first a copy of Samuel Johnson's *Dictionary* at the schoolmistress, Miss Pinkerton, and finally a book of moral precepts at Pitt Crawley. In this adaptation, the wayward actress is triumphant, the audiences are mocked, and the book is defiantly discarded. I would call this a radical adaptation, in all senses: anti-authoritarian, anti-Code and anti-book.

Adaptations in this period gain words, a feature that comes to be seen as the essential ingredient of an adaptation. Many of the adaptations produced in the first decade of sound tend to be victims of their own successes, eclipsed by their later copies and overshadowed by the films made at the end of the decade, 'the golden year' productions of *Gone with the Wind*, *The Wizard of Oz* and *Wuthering Heights*. Where the words are taken from 'classic fiction', the films tend to be marketed as inoffensive, educational, uplifting and conservative. After the success of *All Quiet on the Western Front*, adaptations in this period, on their surfaces at least, seem backward looking in form and style and oblivious to the political context in which they are produced, consigning them to the conservative wing of cinema. However, many of the films discussed in this book demonstrate what Linda Hutcheon argues in *A Theory of Adaptation*: that adaptations 'Return need not be regression'.[23] Indeed, by looking backward, the films are liberated to look forward, appealing to audiences both in agreement and disagreement with the imposition of moral censorship. These films often offer radical challenges to the status quo, perhaps unwittingly, through a conjunction of script, cast, direction and cinematography. In choosing texts that have passed health and safety checks, film-makers, potentially, are able to stretch boundaries much further than

---

[23] Linda Hutcheon (with Siobhan O'Flynn), *A Theory of Adaptation*, 2nd ed. (New York: Routledge, 2013), 175.

when beginning from scratch with new untried narratives.[24] Adaptations in the era of sound, more often than not, are not frightened into silence and are uniquely positioned to take risks, often progressively looking backwards to a silent, more liberated period (*A Tale of Two Cities*), touching upon unjust political expulsion (*A Midsummer Night's Dream*), Christian hypocrisy (*The Barretts of Wimpole Street*) and gender inequality and sexual double standards (*Anna Karenina*), perhaps another reason for why so many of these films were made in a period of increasing repression. These adaptations do not turn backwards to nostalgic recreations of an earlier era but, like Jack Conway's *A Tale of Two Cities*, adapt the stories in 'a period very like the present'.

---

[24] Here I depart from Paul Buhle and Dave Wagner's attribution to the screenwriter alone for the radical content of some Hollywood films. See *Radical Hollywood* (New York: New Press, 2002).

Select Bibliography

Agate, James. *London Pavilion*, no. 768, November 11, 1929.

Alice in Wonderland. Pressbook, 1933.

Altman, Rick. *Film/Genre.* Bassingstoke: Palgrave, 1999.

Anna Karenina. Pressbook, 1935.

Anon. ' "David Copperfield" on the Screen', *The Dickensian* 31: 3 (1935): 223–5.

Anon. '*Oliver Twist Filmed Again*', *The Dickensian*, 29:4 (1933): 302.

Aragay, Mireia, ed. *Books in Motion: Adaptation, Intertextuality, Authorship.* Amsterdam: Rodopi, 2005.

As You Like It. Pressbook, 1936.

Bachelard, Gaston. *The Poetics of Space.* 1958; Boston, MA: Beacon Press, 1994.

Balio, Tino. 'Production Trends.' In *Grand Design: Hollywood as a Modern Business Enterprise 1930–1939*, edited by Tino Balio, 179–312. Berkley: University of California Press, 1993.

Balio, Tino. 'Selling Stars: The Economic Imperative.' In *The Classic Hollywood Reader*, edited by Steve Neale, 209–26. London: Routledge, 2012.

Barr, Charles. 'Two Cities, Two Films.' In *Charles Dickens, A Tale of Two Cities and the French Revolution*, edited by Colin Jones, Josephine McDonagh, and Jon Mee, 166–87. Houndmills: Palgrave, 2009.

Barretts of Wimpole Street. Pressbook, 1934.

Behlmer, Rudy, ed. *Memo from David O. Selznick*, 85–7. New York: Modern Library, 2000.

Bell, Elizabeth, Lynda Haas and Laura Sells, eds. *From Mouse to Mermaid: The Politics of Film, Gender, and Culture.* Bloomington: Indiana University Press, 1995.

Benjamin, Walter. 'The Work of Art in the Age of Mechanical Reproduction.' In *Illuminations*, with an introduction by Hannah Arendt, 211–44. London: Pimlico, 1999.

Bingham, Dennis. *Whose Lives Are They Anyway?: The Biopic as Contemporary Film Genre* New Brunswick, NJ: Rutgers University Press, 2010.

Bluestone, George. *Novels into Film.* Berkeley: University of California Press, 1957.

Boozer, Jack, ed. *Authorship in Film Adaptation.* Austin: University of Texas Press, 2008.

Britton, Andrew. 'Stars and Genres.' In *Stardom: Industry of Desire*, edited by
  Christine Gledhill, 198–206. London: Routledge, 1991.

Brown, Tom, and Belén Vidal, eds. *The Biopic in Contemporary Film Culture.*
  New York: Routledge, 2014.

Buhl, Paul, and Dave Wagner. *Radical Hollywood: The Untold Story.* New York:
  New Press, 2002.

Byrne, Eleanor, and Martin McQuillan. *Deconstructing Disney.* London: Pluto, 1999.

Callow, Simon. *Charles Laughton: A Difficult Actor.* London: Methuen, 1987.

Cartmell, Deborah, ed. *A Companion to Literature, Film and Adaptation.* Oxford:
  Blackwell, 2012.

Cartmell, Deborah. '*Pride and Prejudice* and the Adaptation Genre', *Journal of
  Adaptation in Film & Performance* 3:3 (2010): 227–43.

Cartmell, Deborah, and Imelda Whelehan. *Screen Adaptation: Impure Cinema.*
  Basingstoke: Palgrave, 2010.

Cavell, Stanley. *The World Viewed.* 1971 enlarged edition. Cambridge, MA: Harvard
  University Press, 1979.

Clark, Virginia M. *Aldous Huxley and Film.* London: Scarecrow, 1984.

Crafton, Donald. *The Talkies: American Cinema's Transition to Sound: 1926–1931.*
  Berkley: University of California Press, 1999.

Crowl, Samuel. *Shakespeare and Film.* New York: Norton, 2008.

Custen, George F. *Bio/Pics: How Hollywood Constructed Public History.* New
  Brunswick, NJ: Rutgers University Press, 1992.

David Copperfield. Pressbook, 1935.

DeBona, Guerric. *Film Adaptation in the Hollywood Studio Era.* Urbana: University of
  Illinois Press, 2010.

Desmond, John M., and Peter Hawkes. *Adaptation: Studying Film and Literature.*
  Boston, MA: McGraw-Hill, 2006.

Dexter, Walter. Review of *David Copperfield The Dickensian* 30:3 (1934): 159.

Disraeli. Pressbook, 1934, np.

Doherty, Thomas. *Hollywood and Hitler 1933–1939.* New York: Columbia University
  Press, 2013.

Doherty, Thomas. *Pre-Code Hollywood: Sex, Immorality, and Insurrection in American
  Cinema 1930–34.* New York: Columbia University Press, 1999.

Dr Jeckyll and Mr Hyde. Pressbook, 1931.

Dracula. Pressbook, 1931.

Edwards, Kyle Dawson. 'Poe, You Are Avenged!': Edgar Allan Poe and Universal
  Pictures' *The Raven* (1935)', *Adaptation* 4:2 (2011): 117–36.

Elliott, Kamilla. 'Gothic-Film-Parody', *Adaptation* 1:1 (2008): 24–43.

Elliott, Kamilla. *Rethinking the Novel/Film Debate*. Cambridge: Cambridge University Press, 2003.

Erb, Cynthia. '1931: Movies and the Voice.' In *American Cinema of the 1930s: Themes and Variations*, edited by Ina Rae Hark, 48–68. New Brunswick, NJ: Rutgers University Press, 2007.

Eyman, Scott. *The Speed of Sound*. Baltimore: Johns Hopkins University Press, 1997.

Forsyth, Neil. 'Shakespeare and the Talkies.' In *The Seeming and the Seen: Essays in Modern Visual and Literary Culture*, edited by Beverly Maeder, Jürg Schwyter, Ilona Sigrist, and Boris Vejdovsky, 79–102. Bern: Peter Lang, 2006.

Frankenstein. Pressbook, 1931.

Geduld, Harry M., ed. *Authors on Film*, 68–74. Bloomington: Indiana University Press, 1972.

Geduld, Hary M. *The Birth of the Talkies: From Edison to Jolson*. Bloomington and London: Indiana University Press, 1975.

Genette, Gérard. *Palimpsests*. Translated by Channa Newman and Claude Doubinsky. Lincoln: University of Nebraska Press, 1997.

Geraghty, Christine. 'Foregrounding the Media: *Atonement* (2007) as an Adaptation', *Adaptation* 2:2 (2009): 91–109.

Gifford, Denis. *Books and Plays in Films 1896–1915*. London: McFarland, 1991.

Gomery, Douglas. *The Coming of Sound*. New York: Routledge, 2005.

Gomery, Douglas. *The Hollywood Studio System: A History*. London: BFI, 2005.

Gordon, Jan, and Cora Gordon. *Star-Dust in Hollywood*. London: George G. Harrap & Co., 1930.

Granville-Barker, Harley. 'Alas, Poor Will', *The Listener* XVII 425 (March 3, 1937): 387–9.

Greene, Graham. *Graham Greene: The Pleasure Dome: The Collected Film Criticism 1935–40*, edited by John Russell Taylor, 117–20. London: Secker & Warburg, 1972.

Greene, Graham. *Mornings in The Dark: The Graham Greene Film Reader*, edited by David Parkinson. Manchester: Carcanet, 2007.

Greg, Mank. Commentary on 2002 Warner Bros. Entertainment Inc DVD. *Dr. Jekyll and Mr. Hyde*: 'Two Feature Films on One Disc'.

Hamilton, James Shelley. *National Board of Review Magazine* 13 (1) January 1938, 10–11, reprinted in Anthony Slide, ed. *Selected Film Criticism: 1931–1940, 237–8*. London: Scarecrow Press, 1982.

Heidi. Pressbook, 1937.

Henderson, Diana E. 'A Shrew for the Times, Revisited.' In *Shakespeare the Movie II: Popularizing the Plays on Film, TV, Video and DVD*, edited by Richard Burt and Lydna E. Boose, 120–39. New York: Routledge, 2004.

Higham, Charles Higham. *Charles Laughton: An Intimate Biography*. New York: Doubleday, 1976.

Hilliard, Christopher. *English as a Vocation: The Scrutiny Movement*. Oxford: Oxford University Press, 2012.

Hitchcock, Alfred. 'Much Ado About Nothing.' Reprinted in *Shakespeare on Film, Television and Radio: The Researcher's Guide*, edited by Olwen Terris, Eve-Marie Oesterlen, and Luke McKernan, 45–8. London: British Universities Film & Video Council, 2009.

Hodgdon, Barbara. *The Shakespeare Trade: Performances & Appropriations*. Philadelphia: University of Pennsylvania Press, 1998.

Hunter, William. 'The Art-Form of Democracy?', *Scrutiny* 1:1 (1932): 61–5.

Hutcheon, Linda (with Siobhan O'Flynn). *A Theory of Adaptation*. 2nd ed. New York: Routledge, 2013.

Huxley, Aldous. *Brave New World*. London: Vintage Press, 2004.

Huxley, Aldous. 'Silence is Golden.' In *Authors on Film*, edited by Harry M. Geduld, 68–76. Bloomington: Indiana University Press, 1972.

Jackson, Russell. *Shakespeare & the English-Speaking Cinema*. Oxford: Oxford University Press, 2014.

Jackson, Russell. 'Shakespeare's Comedies on Film.' In *Shakespeare and the Moving Image*, edited by Anthony Davies and Stanley Wells, 99–120. Cambridge: Cambridge University Press, 1994.

Jackson, Russell. *Shakespeare Films in the Making: Vision, Production and Reception*. Cambridge: Cambridge University Press, 2007.

Jacobs, Lea. *The Wages of Sin: Censorship and the Fallen Woman Film, 1928–1942*. Berkley: University of California Press, 1997.

Jones, Maria. ' "His" or "Hers?" The Whips in Sam Taylor's *The Taming of the Shrew*', *Shakespeare Bulletin* 18 (2000): 36–7.

Jorgens, Jack J. *Shakespeare on Film*. Bloomington: Indiana University Press, 1977.

Kavka, Misha. 'Gothic on Screen.' In *The Cambridge Companion to Gothic Fiction*, edited by Jerrold E. Hogle, 209–28. Cambridge: Cambridge University Press, 2002.

Kelly, Andrew. *'All Quiet on the Western Front': The Story of a Film*. London: I.B. Tauris, 1998.

Kael, Pauline. *5001 Nights at the Movies: A Guide from A to Z*. New York: Hot, Rinehart and Winston, 1984.

Lanier, Douglas. *Shakespeare and Modern Popular Culture*. Oxford: Oxford University Press, 2002.

Leavis, F. R., and Denys Thompson. *Culture and Environment*. London: Chatto & Windus, 1933.

Leavis, Q. D. *Fiction and the Reading Public*. 1932; rpt. London: Random House, 2000.

Leitch, Thomas. 'Adaptation and Intertextuality, or What Isn't an Adaptation, and What Does It Matter.' In *A Companion to Literature, Film and Adaptation*, edited by Deborah. Cartmell, 87–104. Oxford: Blackwell, 2012.

Leitch, Thomas. 'Adaptation, the Genre', *Adaptation* 1:2 (2008): 106–20.

Leitch, Thomas. *Film Adaptation and Its Discontents: From 'Gone with the Wind' to 'The Passion of the Christ'*. Baltimore: Johns Hopkins University Press, 2007.

Little Women. Pressbook, 1933.

Love. Pressbook, 1927.

MacQueen, Scott. Audio commentary on *A Midsummer Night's Dream*, 1935, DVD, Turner Entertainment Co and Warner Bros. Entertainment Inc., USA, 2007.

Maltby, Richard. 'The Production Code and the Hays Office.' In *Grand Design: Hollywood as a Modern Business Enterprise, 1930-1939*, edited by Tino Balio, 37–72. Berkeley: University of California Press, 1995.

Manvell, Roger. *Shakespeare & Film*. London: J. M. Dent, 1971.

Marsh, Joss. 'Dickens and Film.' In *The Cambridge Companion to Charles Dickens*, edited by John O. Jordan, 204–29. Cambridge: Cambridge University Press, 2001.

McFarlane, Brian. *Screen Adaptations: Charles Dickens' 'Great Expectations': The Relationship Between Text and Film'* London: Methuen, 2008.

McKernan, Luke an Olwen Terris. *Walking Shadows: Shakespeare in the National Film and Television Archive*. London: BFI, 1994.

Midsummer Night's Dream A. Pressbook, 1935.

Miles, Peter, and Malcolm Smith. *Cinema. Literature & Society*. Beckenham Kent: Croom Helm, 1987.

Monaco, James. *How to Read a Film*. 3rd ed. Oxford: Oxford University Press, 2000.

Murray, Simone. 'Phantom Adaptations: *Eucalyptus*, the Adaptation Industry and the Film that Never Was', *Adaptation* 1:1 (2008). Accessed May 14, 2014. http://adaptation.oxfordjournals.org/content/1/1/5.full

Naremore, James, ed. *Film Adaptation*. New Brunswick, NJ: Rutgers University Press, 2000.

Nicoll, Allardyce. *Film and Theatre*. London: George G. Harrap, 1936.

Ohmer, Susan. '1936: Movies and the Possibility of Transcendence.' In *American Cinema of the 1930s: Themes and Variations*, edited by Ina Rae Hark, 162–81 (New Brunswick, New Jersey and London: Rutgers Univesity Press, 2007).

Oliver Twist. Pressbook, 1933.

Palmer, R. Barton, ed. *Nineteenth-Century American Fiction on Screen*. Cambridge: Cambridge University Press, 2007.

Palmer, R. Barton, ed. *Twentieth-Century American Fiction on Screen*. Cambridge: Cambridge University Press, 2007.

Panofsky, Erwin. 'Style and Medium in the Moving Pictures.' In *Film Theory and Film Criticism: Introductory Essays*, edited by Gerald Mast, Marshall Cohen, and Leo Braudy, 233–48. Oxford: Oxford University Press, 1974.

Pendleton, Thomas A. '*The Taming of the Shrew*, by Shakespeare and Others', *PMLA* 108 (1993): 152–3.

Petrie, Graham. 'Silent Film Adaptations of Dickens: Part II: 1912–1919', *The Dickensian* 97:2 (2001): 101–15.

Private Life of Henry VIII, The. Pressbook, 1933.

Punter, David. 'Introduction: The Ghost of a History.' In *A New Companion to the Gothic*, edited by David Punter, 1–10. Oxford: Wiley-Blackwell, 2012.

Rembrandt. Pressbook, 1937.

Rich Man's Folly. Pressbook, 1931.

Romeo and Juliet. Pressbook, 1936.

Rothwell, Kenneth. *A History of Shakespeare on Screen: A Century of Film and Television*. Cambridge: Cambridge University Press, 1999.

Rubin, Martin. 'Movies and the New Deal in Entertainment.' In *American Cinema of the 1930s: Themes and Variations*, edited by Ina Rae Hark, 92–116. New Brunswick, NJ: Rutgers University Press, 2007.

Sanders, Julie. *Adaptation and Appropriation*. Abingdon: Routledge, 2006.

Schatz, Thomas. *The Genius of the System: Hollywood Film-making in the Studio Era*. London: Random House, 1998.

Schickel, Richard. *The Disney Version: The Life, Times, Art and Commerce of Walt Disney*. 1968; rev. Worcester: Pavilion, 1986.

Scotland, John. *The Talkies*. London: Crosby Lockwood and Son, 1930.

Seldes, Gilbert. *An Hour with the Movies and the Talkies*. London: J.P. Lippincott Co., 1929.

Sennwald, Andre. 'Becky Sharp.' *The New York Times*, June 14, 1935. Accessed August 21, 2014. http://www.nytimes.com/movie/review?res=9C00E1D61139E33ABC4C 52DFB066838E629EDE

Sinyard, Neil. *Filming Literature: the Art of Screen Adaptation*. London: Croom Helm, 1987.

Skal, David J. *Hollywood Gothic: The Tangled Web of 'Dracula' from Novel to Stage to Screen*. 1990; rev. New York: Faber, 2004.

Skal, David. J. *The Monster Show: A Cultural History of Horror*. New York: Norton, 1993.

Slide, Anthony. *Inside the Hollywood Fan Magazine: A History of Star Makers, Fabricators and Gossip Mongers*. Jackson: University Press of Mississippi, 2010.

Slide, Anthony, ed. *Selected Film Criticism: 1931–1940*. London: Scarecrow Press, 1982.

Smoodin, Eric. *Animating Culture: Hollywood Cartoons from the Sound Era*. New Brunswick, NJ: Rutgers University Press, 1993.

Smyth, J. E. 'Hollywood as Historian, 1929-1945.' In *The Wiley-Blackwell History of the American Film, Volume II: 1929–1945*, edited by Cynthia Lucia, Roy Grundmann, and Art Simon, 465–7. Malden, MA: Blackwell, 2012.

Snow White and the Seven Dwarfs. Pressbook, 1948.

Spadoni, Robert. *Uncanny Bodies: The Coming of Sound Film and the Origins of the Horror Genre*. Berkeley: University of California Press, 2007.

Stam, Robert. *Literature Through Film: Realism, Magic, and the Art of Adaptation*. Malden, MA: Blackwell, 2005.

Stam, Robert, and Alessandra Raengo, eds. *A Companion to Literature and Film*. Malden, MA: Blackwell, 2004.

Stam, Robert, and Alessandra Raengo, eds. *Literature and Film: A Guide to the Theory and Practice of Film Adaptation*. Malden, MA: Blackwell, 2005.

Stevens, Jason. 'Insurrection and Depression-Era Politics in Selznick's *A Tale of Two Cities*', *Literature/Film Quarterly* 34:3 (2006): 176–93.

Tale of Two Cities, A. Pressbook, 1935.

Taming of the Shrew, The. Pressbook, 1929.

Thompson, Ann. ed. *The Taming of the Shrew*. Cambridge: Cambridge University Press, 1984.

Turner, A. S. *The Shocking History of Advertising*. London: Penguin, 1952.

Vieira, Mark A. *Hollywood Horror: From Gothic to Cosmic*. New York: Harry N. Abrams, 2003.

Walker, Greg. *The Private Live of Henry VIII*. London: I.B. Tauris, 2003.

Wee Willie Winkie. Pressbook, 1937.

Willson, Robert F. Jr., *Shakespeare in Hollywood 1929–1956*. Madison, NJ: Fairleigh Dickinson University Press, 2000.

Zipes, Jack. *The Enchanted Screen*. New York: Routledge, 2011.

Major Films Discussed

Alice in Wonderland (Paramount, Norman Z. McLeod, 1933)

All Quiet on the Western Front (Universal, Lewis Milestone, 1930)

Anna Christie (MGM, Clarence Brown, 1930)

Anna Karenina (MGM, Clarence Brown, 1935)

As You Like It (Inter-Allied/Twentieth-Century Fox, Paul Czinner, 1936)

Babes in the Wood (Walt Disney Productions/United Artists, Burt Gillett, 1932)

Barretts of Wimpole Street, The. (MGM, Sidney Franklin, 1934)

Becky Sharp (RKO, Rouben Mamoulian, 1935)

Black Cat, The. (Universal, Edgar G. Ulmer, 1934)

Boo (Universal, Albert DeMond, 1932)

Bride of Frankenstein (Universal, James Whale, 1935)

Cleopatra (Paramount, Cecil B. DeMille, 1934)

Country Cousin, The. (United Artists, Wilfred Jackson, 1936)

David Copperfield (MGM, George Cukor, 1935)

Disraeli (Warner Brothers, Alfred E. Green, 1929)

Dr. Jekyll and Mr. Hyde (Paramount, Rouben Mamoulian, 1931)

Dracula (Universal, Tod Browning, 1931)

Frankenstein (Universal, James Whale, 1931)

Freaks (MGM, Tod Browning, 1932)

Great Expectations (Universal, Stuart Walker, 1934)

Great Ziegfeld, The. (Warner Brothers, Robert Z. Leonard, 1936)

Hollywood Revue of 1929, The. (MGM, Charles Reisner, 1929)

Immortal Gentleman, The. (Bernard Smith/Equity British Films, Widgey R. Newman, 1935)

Invisible Man, The. (Universal, James Whale, 1933)

Island of Lost Souls (Paramount, Erle C. Kenton, 1932)

It Happened One Night (Columbia, Frank Capra, 1934)

Jane Eyre (Monogram, Christy Cabanne, 1934)

Jazz Singer, The. (Warner Brothers, Alan Crosland, 1927)

King Kong (RKO, Merian C. Cooper, Ernest B. Schoedsack, 1933)

Klein Dorrit (*Little Dorrit*, Bavaria Film, Carl Lamac, 1934)

Life of Emile Zola, The. (Warner Brothers, William Dieterle, 1937)

Life of Louis Pasteur, The. (Warner Brothers, William Dieterle, 1936)

Little Women (RKO, George Cukor, 1933)

Love (MGM, Edmund Goulding, 1927)

Master Will Shakespeare (MGM, Richard Goldstone, 1936)

Midsummer Night's Dream, A. (Warner Brothers, William Dieterle, Max Reinhardt, 1935)

Mother Goose Goes Hollywood (RKO, Wilfred Jackson, 1938)

Mummy, The. (Universal, Karl Freund, 1933)

Murders in the Rue Morgue (Universal, Robert Florey, 1932)

Mutiny on the Bounty (MGM, Frank Lloyd, 1935)

Mystery of Edwin Drood (Universal, Stuart Walker, 1935)

Mystery of the Wax Museum (Warner Brothers, Michael Curtiz, 1933)

Old Curiosity Shop, The. (British International Pictures, Thomas Bentley, 1934)

Old Dark House, The. (Universal, James Whale, 1932)

Oliver Twist (Monogram, William J. Cowen, 1933)

Private Life of Henry VIII, The. (London Film Productions, Alexander Korda, 1933)

Raven, The. (Universal, Lew Landers, 1935)

Rembrandt (London Film Productions, Alexander Korda, 1936)

Rich Man's Folly (Paramount, John Cromwell, 1931)

Romeo and Juliet (MGM, George Cukor, 1936)

Scrooge (Julius Hagen Productions, Twickenham Film Studios, Henry Edwards, 1935)

Shake, Mr. Shakespeare (Warner Brothers, Roy Mack, 1936)

Show of Shows, The. (Warner Brothers, John G. Adolfi, 1929)

Sign of The Cross, The. (Paramount, Cecil B. DeMille, 1932)

Snow White and the Seven Dwarfs (RKO, William Cottrell, David Hand, Wilfred Jackson, Larry Morey, Perce Pearce and Ben Sharpsteen, 1937)

Story of Temple Drake, The. (Paramount, Stephen Roberts, 1933)

Tale of Two Cities, A. (MGM, Jack Conway, 1935)

Taming of the Shrew (United Artists, Sam Taylor, 1929)

Three Little Pigs, The. (United Artists, Burt Gillett, 1933)

Thru the Mirror (United Artists, David Hand, 1936)

Ugly Duckling, The. (Columbia, Wilfred Jackson, 1931)

Wee Willie Winkie (Twentieth Century Fox, John Ford, 1937)

Who Killed Cock Robin (United Artists, David Hand, 1935)

Index